AAT UNIT 4

Supplying Information for Management Control

STUDY TEXT AND WORKBOOK

Foundation (NVQ/SVQ Level 2)

ISBN 1 84390 549 3

British Library Cataloguing-in-Publication data

A catalogue record for this book is available from the British Library.

We are grateful to the Association of Accounting Technicians for permission to reproduce past assessment materials. The solutions have been prepared by FTC Foulks Lynch.

Published by

FTC Foulks Lynch
Swift House
Market Place
Wokingham
RG40 1AP

All rights reserved. No part of this publication may be reproduced, stored in a retrieval system, or transmitted, in any form or by any means, electronic, mechanical, photocopying, recording or otherwise, without the prior written permission of The Financial Training Company Ltd.

© The Financial Training Company Ltd, 2005

Printed and bound in Great Britain by William Clowes Ltd, Beccles, Suffolk

Contents

	Page
Preface	v
Standards of competence	vii

Study Text

Chapter

		Page
1	Introduction to management information	3
2	Coding of costs and income	13
3	Materials, labour and expenses	19
4	The selling function	37
5	Comparison of information	45
6	Reporting	55
7	Spreadsheets	61
8	Answers to chapter activities	83

Workbook

	Questions	Answers
Key Techniques Question Bank	93	179
Practice Simulation 1	107	191
Answer booklet	119	
Practice Simulation 2	123	195
Answer booklet	131	
Mock Simulation 1	139	199
Answer booklet	155	
Mock Simulation 2	161	205
Answer booklet	173	
Index		211

Preface

This is a study text and workbook for Unit 4 (Supplying Information for Management Control) of the AAT Foundation NVQ/SVQ Level 2 in Accounting.

Study Text

The study text is written in a practical and interactive style:

- key terms and concepts are clearly defined
- all topics are illustrated with practical examples with clearly worked solutions
- frequent practice activities throughout the chapters ensure that what you have learnt is regularly reinforced
- 'pitfalls' and 'examination tips' help you avoid commonly made mistakes and help you focus on what is required to perform well in your simulation.

Icons

Throughout the text we use symbols to highlight the elements referred to above.

 Key facts

 Examination tips and techniques

 Pitfalls

 Practice activities

Workbook

The workbook comprises three main elements:

(a) A question bank of key techniques to give additional practice and reinforce the work covered in each chapter. The questions are divided into their relevant chapters and students may either attempt these questions as they work through the study text, or leave some or all of these until they have completed the study text as a sort of final revision of what they have studied.

(b) Two practice simulations.

(c) Two mock simulations which closely reflect the type of simulation students may expect.

FTC FOULKS LYNCH

Standards of competence

Unit 4 Supplying Information for Management Control

Unit commentary

This unit is about recognising and providing basic management information. This involves information relating to both costs and income and includes the comparison of actual costs and income against the previous period's data, the corresponding period's data and forecast data.

The first element involves recognising cost centres. It should be noted that in some organisations profit centres or investment centres will be used in place of cost centres, and these will differ depending on the organisation. The element also involves recognising elements of costs, coding income and expenditure and identifying and reporting obvious errors, **such as the wrong code or excessive volumes**. You are required to extract information relating to the three elements of costs: materials, labour and expenses. The element, however, does not specifically relate to manufacturing as materials will include items such as consumables in service industries, and the majority of costs will probably be labour costs in those circumstances.

The second element is concerned with extracting information from a particular source, for example the previous period's data, and comparing that information with actual costs and income, in line with the organisational requirements. You are required to report discrepancies between the two in the appropriate format, ensuring confidentiality requirements are adhered to.

Elements contained within this unit are:

Element: 4.1   Code and extract information
Element: 4.2   Provide comparisons on costs and income

Unit 4 Supplying Information for Management Control

Knowledge and understanding

To perform this unit effectively you will need to know and understand:

		Chapter
The business environment		
1	Types of cost centres, including profit centres and investment centres *(Element 4.1)*	1
2	Costs, including wages, salaries, services and consumables *(Element 4.1)*	3
Accounting methods		
3	Identifying cost centres *(Element 4.1)*	1
4	The purpose of management information: decision making; planning and control *(Element 4.1)*	1
5	The make up of gross pay *(Element 4.1)*	3
6	The relationship between financial and management accounting *(Element 4.1)*	1
7	Methods of analysing information in spreadsheets *(Element 4.2)*	7
8	Methods of presenting information, including word-processed documents *(Element 4.2)*	7
9	Handling confidential information *(Element 4.2)*	6
10	The role of management information in the organisation *(Element 4.2)*	1
11	Awareness of the relationship between financial and management accounting *(Element 4.2)*	1
The organisation		
12	Relevant understanding of the organisation's accounting systems and administrative systems and procedures *(Elements 4.1 & 4.2)*	Throughout
13	The nature of the organisation's business transactions *(Elements 4.1 & 4.2)*	
14	The goods and services produced, bought and delivered by the organization *(Element 4.1)*	
15	The cost centres within the organisation *(Element 4.1)*	1, 3
16	Organisational coding structures *(Element 4.1)*	2
17	The organisation's confidentiality requirements *(Element 4.2)*	6
18	House style for presentation of different types of documents, including word-processed documents *(Element 4.2)*	6, 7

Unit 4 Supplying Information for Management Control

Element 4.1 Code and extract information

Performance criteria

In order to perform this element successfully you need to:

A	Recognise appropriate cost centres and elements of costs	1, 3, 4
B	Extract income and expenditure details from the relevant sources	3, 4
C	Code income and expenditure correctly	2, 3, 4
D	Refer any problems in obtaining the necessary information to the appropriate person	3, 4
E	Identify and report errors to the appropriate person	3, 4

Range statement

Performance in this element relates to the following contexts:

Elements of costs:

- Materials
- Labour
- Expenses

Sources:

- Purchase orders
- Purchase invoices
- Sales orders
- Sales invoices
- Policy manual
- Payroll

Information:

- Cost
- Income
- Expenditure

Errors:

- Wrong codes
- Excessive volumes

Unit 4   Supplying Information for Management Control

Element 4.2 Provide comparisons on costs and income

Performance criteria

In order to perform this element successfully you need to:

		Chapter
A	Clarify information requirements with the appropriate person	5
B	Compare information extracted from a particular source with actual results	5
C	Identify discrepancies	5
D	Provide comparisons to the appropriate person in the required format	6
E	Follow organisational requirements for confidentiality strictly	5, 6

Range statement

Performance in this element relates to the following contexts:

Information:

- Costs
- Income

Sources:

- Previous period's data
- Corresponding period's data
- Forecast data
- Ledgers

Format:

- Letter
- Memo
- E-mail
- Note
- Word-processed report

Confidentiality requirements:

- Sharing of information
- Storage of documents

STUDY TEXT

CHAPTER 1

Introduction to management information

Focus

This chapter covers the differences between management accounting and financial accounting and then goes on to look at cost centres, profit centres and investment centres. The chapter then considers the clarification of costs between materials, labour and expenses.

Contents

1. What is a manager?
2. The purpose of management information
3. Management accounting and financial accounting
4. Cost centres
5. Classification of costs

Knowledge and understanding

- Types of cost centre including profit centres and investment centres *(Item 1)*
- Identifying cost centres *(Item 3)*
- The purpose of management information: decision making, planning and control *(Item 4)*
- The relationship between financial and management accounting *(Item 6)*
- The role of management information in the organisation *(Item 10)*
- Awareness of the relationship between financial and management accounting *(Item 11)*
- The cost centres within the organisation *(Item 15)*

Performance criteria

- Recognise appropriate cost centres and elements of cost *(A – element 4.1)*

Key definitions

Financial accounting	The classification and recording of monetary transactions; and the presentation and interpretation of the results of those transactions in order to assess performance over a period and the financial position at a given date.
Cost accounting	The establishment of budgets, standard costs and actual costs of operations, processes, activities or products; and the analysis of variances, profitability or the use of funds.

Management accounting	Aintegral part of management concerned with identifying, presenting and interpreting information used for: formulating strategy, planning and control, decision making, optimising the use of resources and the safeguarding of assets.
Cost centre	Aproduction or service location, function, activity or item of equipment for which costs can be determined.
Profit centre	Aproduction or service location, function or activity for which costs and revenues can be determined.
Investment centre	A production or service location, function or activity for which costs, revenues and net assets can be determined.

1 What is a manager?

A manager in an organisation can include anyone who is involved in the decision-making, planning and controlling of the organisation. There are different levels of management, for example the managing director is at a higher level than the line manager of the production department, therefore the information requirements of these managers will be different.

2 The purpose of management information

Managers need useful information in order to make decisions, to plan and to control the company. **Management accountants** provide managers with this information.

2.1 Decision-making

In the course of running a business, management will be faced with many decisions. These will cover both **long-term decisions** about the future direction of the business and **short-term decisions** about the day-to-day running of the organisation.

Examples of **long-term** decisions that managers may make include:

(a) which products to continue to produce and sell based upon the profitability and market share of those products

(b) which products to withdraw from manufacturing and selling

(c) how many staff to employ – whether there should be a reduction in the number of employees or more staff should be recruited

(d) whether or not to invest in new machinery and equipment.

Other **day-to-day** decisions that might have to be made include:

(e) which products to make and how many to make each production run

(f) how much overtime is required

(g) how much stock to hold

(h) how frequently orders for raw materials should be placed.

Management information supplies managers with the information that will allow them to make informed decisions on these matters.

INTRODUCTION TO MANAGEMENT INFORMATION : CHAPTER 1

Activity 1 *(There is no feedback to this activity)*

Think about the kind of decisions that get made in your organisation or somewhere you have worked in the past. Which were long-term decisions and which were day-to-day decisions?

2.2 Planning

The management of an organisation will spend much of its time looking forward and planning the longer-term operations and strategy of the organisation. In order to be able to plan how to successfully operate the organisation in the future, managers will need current, detailed information about the organisation.

Management will need to make detailed plans. These plans may include how many of each type of product to make and sell, what these products will cost to make, how many employees are required to make the products and how much they must be paid, how many employees are needed to support the production process and how much this will cost, what other costs will be incurred. These detailed plans are known as **budgets**.

Definition   Budgets are plans set in financial and/or quantitative terms for either the whole of a business or parts of a business for a specified period of time in the future, usually one year.

In order to prepare these budgets, managers will need to know what each product costs to manufacture or how much it costs to provide a particular service to customers in order to decide which products or services to continue. They will need to know how productive the various employees or work groups are in order to concentrate efforts on improving productivity. They will need to know how much has been spent on advertising in the past in order to determine how much should be spent in the future.

2.3 Control

As well as making plans for the future management will also be concerned with how well the organisation has achieved its targets and plans that were made in previous periods. Management must be able to control costs, expenses and income by constant comparison of actual costs and income to those that were anticipated in earlier budgets.

3 Management accounting and financial accounting

Accounting information provides managers of an organisation with information to help them with:

Planning – e.g. sales forecasts, future raw material costs

Controlling – e.g. variances, stock levels

Decision-making – e.g. product costs, departmental productivity.

Financial accounting information and **management accounting** information will come from the same sources, they will simply be presented differently.

3.1 Financial accounting

The **financial accounts** record transactions between the business and its customers, suppliers, employees and owners. The managers of the business must account for the way in which funds entrusted to them have been used and, therefore, records of assets and liabilities are needed as well as a statement of any increase in the total wealth of the business. Financial accounts are presented in the form of a **profit and loss account** and **balance sheet**.

FTC FOULKS LYNCH

Definition   Financial accounting is:

- the classification and recording of monetary transactions; and
- the presentation and interpretation of the results of those transactions in order to assess performance over a period and the financial position at a given date.

3.2 Cost accounting

Cost accounting involves applying a set of principles, methods and techniques to determine and analyse costs within the separate units of a business.

Definition   The establishment of budgets, standard costs and actual costs of operations, processes, activities or products; and the analysis of variances, profitability or the use of funds.

3.3 Management accounting

Management accounting is a wider concept involving **professional knowledge and skill** in the preparation and presentation of information to all levels of management in an organisation. The source of such information is the financial and cost accounts. The information is intended to assist management in decision-making, planning and control activities in both the short and long term.

Definition   An integral part of management concerned with identifying, presenting and interpreting information used for: formulating strategy, planning and control, decision making, optimising the use of resources and the safeguarding of assets.

3.4 Involvement with management

Financial accounting, cost accounting and management accounting involve participation in management to ensure that there is effective:

- formulation of plans to meet objectives
- formulation of short term operations plans
- acquisition and use of finance and recording of actual transactions
- communication of financial and operating information
- corrective action to bring plans and results into line
- reviewing and reporting on systems and operations.

3.5 Financial accounts and management information

It may be helpful to look at a simple profit and loss account to see the role of management accounting:

XYZ Company
Profit and loss account for period X

	£	£
Sales		200,000
Cost of sales:		
Materials consumed	80,000	
Wages	40,000	
Production expenses	15,000	
		135,000
Gross profit		65,000

Marketing expenses	15,000	
General administrative expenses	10,000	
Financing costs	4,000	
	------	29,000

Net profit		36,000

This statement may be adequate to provide outsiders with an overview of the trading results of the whole business, but managers would need much more detail to answer questions such as:

- What are the major products and are they profitable?
- How much have stocks of raw materials increased?
- How does labour cost per unit compare with the last period?
- Are personnel department expenses more than expected?

The management accounting system reports will provide the answers to these (and many other) questions on a regular basis. In addition, the management accounts will contain detailed information concerning stocks of raw materials, work in progress and finished goods as a basis for the valuation necessary to prepare periodic and final accounts.

3.6 Cost accounting system

The cost accounting system is the **entire system of documentation**, accounting records and personnel that provide periodic cost accounts and cost information for management as part of the management reporting system.

3.7 Benefits of cost accounting

The main benefit is the provision of information that can be used specifically to:

- disclose profitable and unprofitable activities
- identify waste and inefficiency
- analyse movements in profit
- estimate and fix selling prices
- value stocks
- develop budgets and standards to assist planning and control
- evaluate the cost effects of policy decisions.

Thus, by a **detailed analysis** of expenditure, costing becomes an important element of **managerial planning and control**.

3.8 The relationship between management and financial information

Financial accounting information and management information come from the same sources but are presented differently. For example the cost of purchases for a week will be found in the financial accounting records from the purchases day book posted to the purchases account. The original information for the primary records would have come from the purchase invoices.

For management information purposes it may be more useful for the purchases of each different type of raw material to be identified. Again, the information will come from the purchase invoices but instead of a single total for purchases this will be broken down into each raw material.

With all of the different costs of a business, materials, labour and expenses the information that is recorded in the financial accounting records will be same as that recorded in the management accounting records. The only difference will be in the way in which the information is classified and presented.

4 Cost centres

4.1 Classification and analysis of costs

Classification is a means of analysing costs into logical groups so that they can be summarised into meaningful information for management use or for preparing external financial reports.

Management will require information to make decisions on a variety of issues, each of which may require different cost summaries, for example costs may be required for a particular product, or for a department, or for the organisation as a whole.

4.2 Cost centres

Definition A cost centre is a production or service location, function, activity or item of equipment for which **costs** can be determined.

A **cost centre** is a 'part of the business' to which costs can be related, for example, a paint manufacturer cost centres might be:

- mixing department
- packaging department
- stores
- maintenance
- canteen
- administration
- selling and marketing departments.

The mixing and packaging departments **production** cost centres as the paint is actually made here. The others are **service** cost centres as they provide additional services required by the organisation.

For an accountancy practice, a service organisation, the cost centres might be:

- audit
- taxation
- accountancy
- word processing
- administration
- canteen
- various geographical locations e.g. the London office, the Reading office, the Edinburgh office.

Determining the total cost for each cost centre is important for:

- relating costs to cost units
- planning future costs
- controlling costs, i.e. comparing either actual to budgeted, or actual cost to 'buy in'.

Therefore, a **cost centre manager** is responsible only for cost.

Activity 2 *(There is no feedback to this activity)*

Try to list the cost centres in your company, or think about a company you know well and what their cost centres might be.

4.3 Profit centres

Definition A profit centre is a production or service location, function or activity for which **costs and revenues** can be determined.

Thus a profit centre is a **responsibility centre**, similar to a cost centre, but has identifiable revenues as well as costs.

For a paint manufacturer profit centres might be a specific site or factory. For an accountancy practice the profit centres might be the individual locations or the type of business undertaken (audit, consultancy, accountancy etc). Clearly all profit centres can also be cost centres, but not all cost centres can be profit centres.

Determining the excess of revenue over cost for each profit centre is important for:

(a) planning future profits
(b) controlling costs and revenues, i.e. comparing actual to budget
(c) measuring management performance.

The **manager of a profit centre** is therefore accountable for costs, revenues and profit.

4.4 Investment centres

Definition An investment centre is a production or service location, function or activity for which **costs, revenues and net assets** can be determined.

Therefore an investment centre is similar to a profit centre but as well as having identifiable costs and revenues it also has identifiable assets and liabilities.

For our paint manufacturer this could be a group of sites or factories. For the accountancy practice the Edinburgh office and the London office.

An **investment centre manager** is therefore accountable for costs, revenues, profit and assets employed.

Conclusion A **cost centre** is a part of the organisation for which costs can be determined.

A **profit centre** is a part of the organisation for which costs and revenues, therefore profit, can be determined.

An **investment centre** is a sector of the organisation for which costs, revenues and net assets can be determined.

5 Classification of costs

Costs are not only analysed and classified according to the cost centre or profit centre or investment centre that they relate to but also according the type of cost. For basic management accounting purposes there are three types of classification of costs:

- Materials
- Labour
- Expenses

5.1 Materials

Materials costs are the costs of the purchases of raw materials that are to be used in the manufacturing process in a manufacturing organisation or alternatively the cost of goods that are to be resold in a retail organisation.

For management accounting purposes it is important to record information about the materials purchases. This information will be provided by the purchase invoice for the materials. The type of information required will include:

- The quantity of each type of material and its unit cost for the stores records
- The cost of raw materials used by each cost centre.

Example

A business manufactures children's wooden toys in an assembly cost centre, where the toys are put together, and a finishing cost centre, where they are painted or polished. An invoice has been received from a supplier for the following items:

20 metres birch wood	£16.80 per metre	£336.00
40 litres red wood paint	£2.40 per litre	£ 96.00
Goods total		£432.00
VAT	17.5%	£ 75.60
Invoice total		£507.60

The information from this invoice would be used as follows:

- The stores records would be updated to show the receipt of 20 metres of birch wood and 40 litres of red paint
- The assembly cost centre would be charged with £336.00 of materials and the finishing cost centre would be charged with £96.00 of materials (the VAT will be charged to a separate account)

Materials costs are considered in more detail in a later chapter.

5.2 Labour

The information for labour costs will come from the payroll records. The costs of these employees are then charged to the cost centre which has used their time. Labour costs can consist of not only basic pay but overtime, commissions and bonuses as well.

Labour costs will be considered in more detail in a later chapter.

5.3 Expenses

The final category of costs is that of expenses which are sometimes also known as overheads. These are all of the other types of costs incurred by an organisation other than materials and labour costs. There will include such costs are rent, rates, heat and power costs, cleaning costs, advertising expenses etc.

Expenses will be considered in more detail in a later chapter.

5.4 Service industries

The classification of costs between materials, labour and expenses considered in outline above relates largely to a manufacturing type of organisation. However a service organisation will have similar categorisations of costs. A service organisation which provides a service rather than a product will tend to have large amounts of labour costs and expenses rather than the materials purchased by a manufacturing organisation. However service industries will still require types of materials such as stationary, computer discs etc which tend to be called **consumables**.

Activity 3 *(The answer is in the final chapter of this study text)*

Murray plc has two departments – one produces cakes and the other produces tablecloths. The following expenses have been incurred this month:

1 tonne chocolate chips	£150
3 hours of a cake decorator's time	£60
Rent of the Murray plc building	£1,000
300 metres of purple cotton	£2,500
2 sewing machine operators working 40 hours each	£800
Cardboard cake boxes	£40
Electricity bill for whole company	£220

Classify each of these costs according to whether they are materials, labour or expenses.

---

6 Quick quiz *(The answer is in the final chapter of this study text)*

1. What are the three main tasks of management in an organisation?
2. What is a cost centre?
3. What is a profit centre?
4. What are the three main classifications of costs?

7 Summary

This introductory chapter has set the scene for further studies of management information. You should now know how management information differs from financial accounting information. You should also understand what is meant by cost centres, profit centres and investment centres and the basic type of classification of costs.

CHAPTER 2

Coding of costs and income

Focus

This chapter looks at the use of coding in organisation, including how income and expenditure is coded.

Contents

1 Classification and coding of costs
2 Coding of costs in practice
3 Coding income
4 Problems with coding

Knowledge and understanding

- Organisational coding structures *(Item 16)*

Performance criteria

- Code income and expenditure correctly *(C – element 4.1)*

Key definition

Code A system of symbols designed to be applied to a classified set of items, to give a brief accurate reference, which helps entry to the records, collation and analysis.

---

1 Classification and coding of costs

Cost accountants need to determine the costs that relate to each cost centre. To make this simpler, each expense is classified according to its cost centre and type of expense. A **cost code** is then allocated to the expense to represent this classification.

1.1 Cost codes

Definition A **code** is a system of symbols designed to be applied to a classified set of items, to give a brief accurate reference, which helps entry to the records, collation and analysis.

A cost code is a code used in a costing system.

The first step in creating a cost code will be to determine the cost centre to which the cost relates and then to allocate the correct cost centre code.

Example

If a cost relates to Machine Group 7 the cost centre code might be 07. If the cost relates to the canteen the cost centre code might be 16.

1.2 Generic or functional code

Once a cost has been allocated its correct cost centre code then it may also be useful to know the particular type of expense involved. Therefore some more digits might be added to the cost centre code to represent the precise type of cost.

Example

If an expense for Machine Group 7 is for oil then its code might be 07 (for its cost centre) followed by 23 to represent materials.

If an expense of the canteen is identified as frozen peas then its cost code might be 16 (its cost centre) followed by 02 to represent food purchases (materials).

1.3 Specific code

Finally it may be necessary for cost allocation, decision making or accounting purposes to allocate a code which specifically identifies the item of cost.

Example

The oil for Machine Group 7 might eventually be coded as:

072304

This represents Machine Group 7 (07) material use (23) of oil (04).

The frozen peas for the canteen might be coded as:

160219

This represents canteen (16) food purchases (02) of frozen peas (19).

Conclusion   A cost code is designed to analyse and classify the costs of an organisation in the most appropriate manner for that organisation. Therefore there are no set methods of designing a cost code and the cost code of a particular organisation will be that which best suits the operations and costs of that business.

Activity 1 *(The answer is in the final chapter of this study text)*

Suppose that a cost coding system is such that the first two letters of the code represent the cost centre, the third letter the type of expense and the fourth letter the detail of the expense.

Codes are as follows:

S	Salesman's expenses
ED	Eastern Division
P	Petrol

Code an Eastern Division's salesman's petrol expenses.

1.4 Purpose of cost codes

The main purposes of cost codes are to:

- **assist precise information**: costs incurred can be associated with pre-established codes, so reducing variations in classification

- **facilitate electronic data processing**: computer analysis, summarisation and presentation of data can be performed more easily through the use of codes

- **facilitate a logical and systematic arrangement of costing records**: accounts can be arranged in blocks of codes permitting additional codes to be inserted in logical order

- **simplify comparison of totals of similar expenses** rather than all of the individual items

- **incorporate check codes** within the main code to check the accuracy of the postings.

Example

Owen Ltd manufactures motorbike helmets.

It has four sales areas and two factories that are coded as:

Scotland and the North	100
Midlands	101
South East	102
South West	103

Factories:

Slough	110
Leeds	111

Cost centres:

Machining	120
Finishing	121
Packing	122
Stores	123
Canteen	124
Maintenance	125
Administration	126

Type of expense:

Labour	200
Material	201
Expenses	202

Sales revenue: 210

Thus, the cost of production labour in the Finishing Department at the Leeds factory would be coded 111/121/200.

UNIT 4 : SUPPLYING INFORMATION FOR MANAGEMENT CONTROL

Activity 2 *(The answer is in the final chapter of this study text)*

The following is a list of costs related to the business activity. Code these using the structure above:

(i) Slough factory, cleaning materials used in the canteen

(ii) Slough factory, wages for stores personnel

(iii) Leeds factory, metered power (electricity) for Machining Department

(iv) Leeds factory, telephone account for site as a whole

(v) Sales from Slough factory to customer in Exeter

(vi) Slough factory, general maintenance material for repairs.

2 Coding of costs in practice

2.1 Timing of coding

In order to be of most use the coding of costs should take place when the cost or expense is first received by the organisation. In most cases this will be when the invoice for the goods is received.

After this point the documents will be entered into the accounting system and then to the filing system so it is important that the coding is done immediately.

2.2 Receiving an invoice

When an invoice is received by the organisation it will undergo a variety of checks to ensure that it is for valid purchases that were ordered and have been received or that it is for a service that has been received. In the process of these checks it will become clear what type of goods or service is being dealt with, for example it may be an invoice for the purchase of raw materials for the factory or an electricity bill for the entire organisation.

Once the invoice has been checked for validity then it must be correctly coded.

2.3 Choosing the correct code

In order for the correct code to be given to the invoice, it is vital that the person responsible for the coding fully understands the nature of the organisation and the costs that it incurs. The organisation's coding listing should be referred to and the correct cost centre, type and expense code should be entered on the front of the invoice.

2.4 Indirect costs

Some costs, for example electricity bills, cannot be allocated directly to a single cost centre as they are indirect costs. Eventually a portion of this electricity bill will be shared out to each of the cost centres that uses electricity but at the point where the account is being coded it must simply be recognised that this is a shared cost and not a cost that should be coded to a particular cost centre.

Therefore, the coding structure of the organisation should include some codes that specifically identify a cost as a shared cost.

2.5 Cheque and cash payments

As well as receiving invoices for costs incurred on credit most organisations will also write cheques for costs and even pay some costs out of petty cash. These costs must be coded in just the same way as expenses on credit.

If the payment is by cheque then there will be some documentation to support that payment. When this documentation is authorised for payment then it should also be coded for costing purposes.

If payments are made out of petty cash then they must be supported by a petty cash voucher. Again this voucher must be coded according to the type of cost.

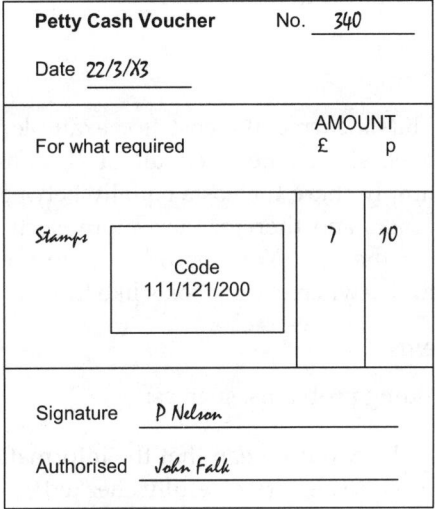

2.6 Payment of wages and salaries

Wages and salaries normally form a very large part of the costs incurred by an organisation. If wages or salaries are paid by cheque or in cash then the supporting documentation, the payslip, should be coded as with other cash payments. However frequently wages and salaries will usually be paid directly into employee's bank accounts through the BACS system. Therefore it is important that the wages and salaries costs are coded according to the department or cost centre so that the total labour cost of the cost centre is known.

3 Coding income

If an organisation has profit or investment centres then the income of the organisation must also be correctly coded.

3.1 Sales invoices

If an organisation makes sales on credit then when the sales invoice is raised it should be coded according to the coding listing. This code will probably specify the profit centre or investment centre that has made the sale and often also the product that is being sold.

3.2 Cash sales

In a retail organisation sales may be made for cash. There should always be documentation that supports the cash takings, such as the till rolls for the day. This documentation then needs to be coded to reflect the profit or investment centre that made the sales and any other detailed product coding that is required by the organisation. Most modern cash registers will automatically code each sale.

4 Problems with coding

4.1 Which code?

The main problem when coding documents is deciding which cost centre and analysis code to use; the documents may not clearly show which cost centre incurred the costs or the type of cost it is.

If you are unable to code a document try:

- looking in the organisations procedure book

- referring the query document to your supervisor.

4.2 Apportionment

If more than one cost centre has incurred the cost (for example, a heating bill for the whole building), the cost needs to be shared between all of the cost centres (or **apportioned**). Although it may be easy to simply share the costs equally between the cost centres, some cost centres may be bigger than others and therefore use more electricity/heating etc – so should receive a greater percentage of the cost. You should refer to your organisation's procedures book or your supervisor for advice when coding costs like this.

4.3 Other coding problems

You may come across other coding problems, such as:

1   The wrong code used: this would mean that the information on the accounting system is also wrong. Codes need to be very carefully checked.

2   The wrong organisation: occasionally, an invoice might arrive that is for a company with a similar name or address. You should check invoice details carefully so that errors like this don't get entered on to the accounting system.

5 Quick quiz *(The answer is in the final chapter of this study text)*

1   Define the term 'cost code'.

2   List three purposes of cost codes.

3   How are costs coded in practice?

6 Summary

You should now know the importance of coding of costs and income. If actual costs and income are to be used for management purposes then it is vital that they are correctly classified and coded to ensure that they are allocated to the correct cost, profit or investment centre. Only then can any useful management information be obtained.

CHAPTER 3

Materials, labour and expenses

Focus

This chapter considers in more detail the three main cost classifications of material, labour and expenses.

Contents

1. Materials control cycle
2. Labour costs
3. Calculating gross pay – time related pay
4. Calculating gross pay – output related pay
5. Bonus schemes
6. Payroll
7. Non-manufacturing organisations
8. Expenses
9. Cost centres and expenses

Knowledge and understanding

- Costs including wages, salaries and consumables *(Item 2)*
- The make up of gross pay *(Item 5)*
- The cost centres within the organisation *(Item 15)*

Performance criteria

- Recognise appropriate cost centres and elements of costs *(A – element 4.1)*
- Extract income and expenditure details from the relevant sources *(B – element 4.1)*
- Code income and expenditure correctly *(C – element 4.1)*
- Refer any problems in obtaining the necessary information to the appropriate person *(D – element 4.1)*
- Identify and report errors to the appropriate person *(E – element 4.1)*

Key definitions

Purchase requisition	A request for materials required by a cost centre
Purchase order	An order placed with a supplier for an agreed quantity of materials at an agreed price

Delivery note	Sent by the supplier of goods with the goods on delivery
Goods received note	Completed by the receiving company to record the details and quantity of goods delivered
Purchase invoice	Request from the supplier of goods for payment under the agreed terms
Bin card	Record of receipts, issues and balances of stock in hand kept by the store keeper
Goods requisition note	Record of materials issued to production departments
Goods returned note	Record of unused materials returned to the stores department
Direct materials	Materials actually used to make the products
Indirect materials	Other materials that are used but are not directly part of the product that is being made
Clock card	A document which records the starting and finishing time for an employee
Time sheet	A record of how a person's time at work has been spent
Job sheet	Records the number of each type of product that n employee has produced in the period
Overtime	The number of hours worked by an employee which is greater than the number of hours set by the organisation as the working week
Overtime premium	The amount over and above the normal hourly rate that employees are paid for overtime hours
Direct labour	The employees who work directly on making the products of the organisation
Indirect labour	Other employees who do not directly make any of the products
Expenses	All business costs that are not classified as materials or labour costs
Allocation	Expenses are directly attributed to a single cost centre that incurred them
Apportionment	Any joint expenses are split up in some equitable manner between each cost centre that has incurred some of these expenses

1 Materials control cycle

1.1 Introduction

Materials can often form the largest single item of cost for a business so it is essential that the material purchased is the most suitable for the intended purpose.

1.2 Control of purchasing

When goods are purchased they must be ordered, received by the stores department, recorded, issued to the manufacturing department that requires them and eventually paid for. This process needs a great deal of paperwork and strict internal controls.

Internal control consists of full documentation and appropriate authorisation of all transactions, movements of materials and of all requisitions, orders, receipts and payments.

If control is to be maintained over purchasing, it is necessary to ensure that:

- only necessary items are purchased

- orders are placed with the most appropriate supplier after considering price and delivery details

- the goods that are actually received are the goods that were ordered and in the correct quantity

- the price paid for the goods is correct (i.e. what was agreed when the order was placed).

To ensure that all of this takes place requires a reliable system of checking and control.

1.3 Overview of procedures

It is useful to have an overview of the purchasing process.

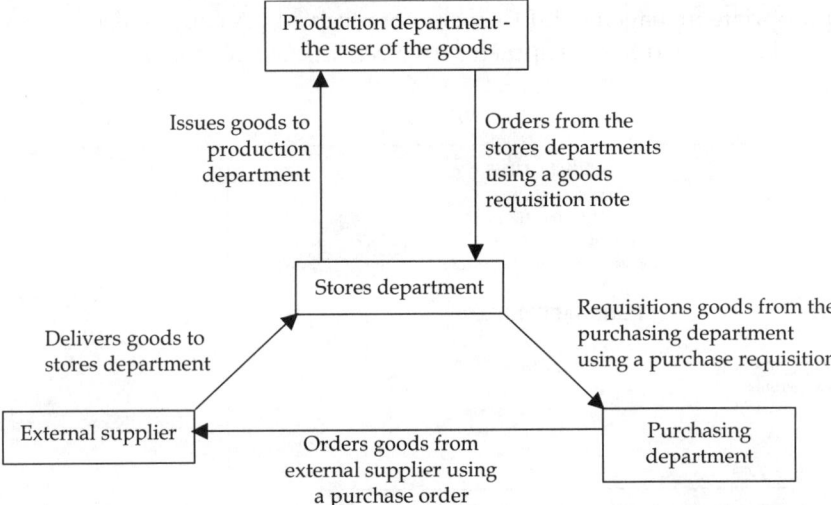

There are many variations of the above system in practice, but it is a fairly typical system and does provide good control over the purchasing and issuing process.

Activity 1 *(There is no feedback to this activity)*

Your organisation may have a slightly different process to this. See if you can draw a similar diagram illustrating the way your organisation's (or a familiar organisation's) purchasing process works.

1.4 Purchase requisition

It is important that an organisation controls the goods that are ordered from suppliers. Only goods that are genuinely necessary should be ordered. Therefore, before any order for goods is placed, a purchase requisition must be completed.

Each purchase requisition must be authorised by the appropriate person. This will usually be the storekeeper or store manager.

When the purchase requisition has been completed it is sent to the purchasing department so that the purchase order is prepared.

UNIT 4 : SUPPLYING INFORMATION FOR MANAGEMENT CONTROL

1.5 Purchase order

Purchase orders will be placed with suppliers by the purchasing department. The choice of supplier will depend upon the price, delivery promise, quality of goods and past performance.

The person placing the order must first check that the purchase requisition has been authorised by the appropriate person in the organisation.

Once the supplier of the goods has been chosen, the purchase price of the goods must be determined. This will either be from the price list of the supplier or from a special quotation of the price by that supplier. The price agreed will be entered on the purchase order together with details of the goods being ordered.

The purchase order must then be authorised by the appropriate person in the organisation before being dispatched to the supplier.

A copy of the purchase order is sent to the goods receiving department or stores department as confirmation of expected delivery. The goods receiving department therefore know that goods are due and can alert appropriate management if they are not received. A copy is also sent to the accounts department to be matched to the supplier's invoice. An example purchase order is show below.

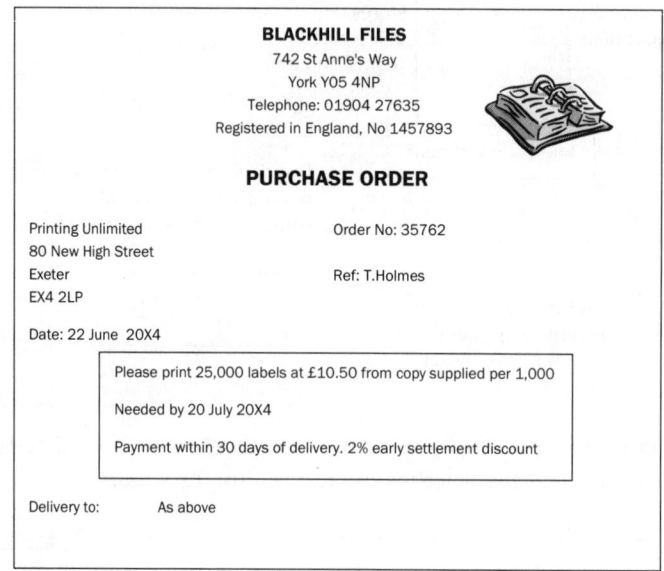

1.6 Delivery note

A delivery note is sent by the supplier with the goods being delivered. This must include full details of the goods being delivered. The delivery note is signed by the person receiving the goods as evidence that the goods arrived.

1.7 Goods received note

When goods are received by the organisation they will usually be taken to a central goods receiving department or stores department rather than being delivered directly to the part of the organisation that will use the goods. This enables the receipt of goods to be controlled.

The goods receiving department or stores department have copies of all purchase orders. It is important that the goods that arrive actually agree in **all** detail to those ordered before they are accepted.

When the goods are received, the stores department will firstly check what the goods are. They will be identified and counted and the supplier and purchase order to which they relate will be identified.

The details of the delivery note are checked to the actual goods and to the purchase order. It is important that the stores department checks that these goods were actually ordered by the organisation before accepting them.

Finally, when the stores department are satisfied with all of the details of the delivery, the details are recorded on a goods received note (GRN).

Any concerns about the goods being delivered (for example, too few, too many, the wrong colour, the wrong size) should be referred immediately to the appropriate manager before accepting the goods.

The GRN is evidence that the goods that were ordered have been received and therefore should be, and can be, paid for. The GRN will, therefore, be sent to the accounts department to be matched with the supplier's invoice.

As evidence of the actual receipt of the goods the GRN is also used for entering receipts of materials in the stores records.

1.8 Purchase invoice

The purchase invoice for goods details the amount that the receiver of the goods must pay for them and the date that payment is due. The purchase invoice might be included when the goods themselves are delivered, or might be sent after delivery.

The person responsible for payment must check that the details of the purchase invoice agree to the goods received note, the delivery note and the purchase order. This is to ensure that:

- what was ordered was received
- what was received is what is being paid for
- the price charged is that agreed.

Once it is certain that the purchase invoice agrees with the goods that were actually received then the invoice can be authorised for payment by the appropriate person in the organisation.

1.9 Bin cards

The storekeeper must know at any time how much of any item he has in stock. This is done by use of a bin card.

Definition A **bin card** is a simple record of receipts, issues and balances of stock in hand kept by storekeepers, recorded in quantities of materials stock.

The bin card is a duplication of the quantity information recorded in the stores ledger (see later in this chapter) but storekeepers frequently find that such a ready record is a very useful aid in carrying out their duties.

An example of a bin card for an item of stock is given overleaf.

BIN CARD

Description ..Chipboard.............. Location ..Stores.............. Code ..D35..........

Maximum ..3,000m.... Minimum ..1,000m.... Reorder level ..1,400m.... Reorder quantity ..200m........

Receipts			Issues			Current stock level	On order		
Date	GRN Ref	Quantity	Date	Issue Ref	Quantity		Date	Ref	Quantity
30/7/X3	8737	200m				200m	01/8/X3	PO6752	300m
06/8/X3	8748	300m				500m			
			07/8/X9	3771	400m				

The bin card does not have value columns.

1.10 Goods requisition note

Materials issued to production departments from the stores department are controlled by a goods requisition note (also referred to as a stores requisition). This document authorises the storekeeper to release the goods to the production department.

1.11 Goods returned note

When unused materials are returned from user departments to the stores, the transaction will be recorded on a document similar to the materials requisition but usually printed in a different colour. This will be a goods returned note. It will be completed by the user department that is returning the goods and signed by the storekeeper as evidence that the goods were returned to stores.

When the goods are returned the details on the goods returned note must be checked to the actual goods themselves.

1.12 Summary of documents used

Purchase requisition

- filled out by stores
- authorised
- sent to purchasing department.

Purchase order

- filled out by purchasing department
- supplier chosen by purchasing department
- price of goods calculated from price list
- authorised
- sent to supplier.

Delivery note

- provided by supplier with delivery
- received together with goods by stores department
- compared to actual goods
- goods checked and counted
- delivery note and goods checked to purchase order.

Goods received note

- a document produced by stores department for their own use
- goods checked and counted
- written up and signed
- matched with delivery note and purchase order
- sent to accounts to await purchase invoice.

Purchase invoice

- received from supplier
- checked to purchase order, delivery note and goods received note authorised for payment
- authorised for payment
- payment made.

Stores requisition note

- filled out by user department
- authorised
- sent to stores.

Goods returned note

- filled out by returning department
- actual goods checked against goods returned note by stores
- signed as evidence of receipt.

Bin card

- maintained by stores department
- written up from goods received note, goods requisition note and goods returned note
- shows quantity of goods held in stores.

1.13 Stores ledger account

Earlier in this section we saw that the quantity of each item of stock was recorded by the storekeeper on a bin card. The accounts department also keep records for each line of stock, both quantity and value, and this is known as the **stores ledger account**.

Definition A stores ledger account records the quantity and value of receipts and issues and the current balance of each item of stock.

The stores ledger account for the item of stock recorded in the bin card earlier in this section is give below:

STORES LEDGER ACCOUNT

Material Chipboard

Code D35

	Receipts				Issues				Balance		
Date	GRN No	Qty	Price per unit £	Amount £	Material requisition	Qty per unit	Price £	Amount £	Qty per unit	Price £	Value £
30/7/X3	8737	200m	2.00	400.00					200	2.00	400.00
06/8/X3	8748	300m	2.00	600.00					500	2.00	1,000.00
07/8/X3					3771	400m	2.00	800.00	100	2.00	200.00

1.14 Direct and indirect materials

Within the category of materials they can also be classified for management accounting purposes as either **direct materials** or **indirect materials**.

Definition **Direct** materials are the materials that are used directly as part of the production of the goods that the organisation makes.

The direct materials are therefore the raw materials that are part of the manufacturing process. In a business that makes wooden furniture the direct materials would for example include wood, hinges and polish.

Definition **Indirect** materials are other materials used in the production process which are not used in the actual products themselves.

So for example lubricant for the machines that make the wooden furniture would be classified as indirect materials.

2 Labour costs

2.1 Documentation and procedures to record labour costs

When an employee joins an organisation it must record details of the employee, their job and pay. This is done by the personnel department in the individual employee's personnel record.

Details that might be kept about an employee are as follows:
- full name, address and date of birth
- personal details such as marital status and emergency contact name and address
- National Insurance number
- previous employment history
- educational details
- professional qualifications
- date of joining organisation
- employee number or code
- clock number issued
- job title and department
- rate of pay agreed
- holiday details agreed
- bank details if salary is to be paid directly into bank account
- amendments to any of the details above (such as increases in agreed rates of pay)
- date of termination of employment (when this takes place) and reasons for leaving.

2.2 Employee record of attendance

On any particular day an employee may be at work, on holiday, absent due to sickness or absent for some other reason. A record must be kept of these details for each day.

This information about an employee's attendance will come from various sources such as clock cards, time sheets, job sheets, and job cards.

2.3 Holiday

Employees have an agreed number of days holiday per year. This will usually be paid holiday for salaried employees but may well be unpaid for employees paid by results or on time rates.

It is important for the employer to keep a record of the days of holiday taken by the employee to ensure that the agreed number of days per year are not exceeded.

2.4 Sickness

The organisation will have its own policies regarding payment for sick leave as well as legal requirements for statutory sick pay. Therefore, it is necessary to keep a record of the number of days of sick leave each year for each employee.

2.5 Other periods of absence

A record needs to be kept of any other periods of absence by an employee. These might be perfectly genuine such as jury service or training courses or alternatively unexplained periods of absence that must be investigated.

2.6 Clock cards

Definition A **clock card** is a document which records the starting and finishing time for an employee. (for example, 9 til 5.30)

There is usually some form of electronic or computerised recording system, so that when the employee's clock card is entered into the machine the time is recorded. This will give the starting and finishing time for the day and also in some systems break times taken as well. Not all organisations will have these; you probably will never come across them! They are mainly used in **factories** for shift work.

Clock cards are used as a source document in the calculation of the employee's gross pay.

2.7 Time sheets

Definition A **time sheet** is a record of how a person's time at work has been spent.

The total hours that an employee has worked in a day or week are known from the employee's clock card but a breakdown of how those hours were spent is shown on the time sheet.

In some organisations, each employee fills out a time sheet on a daily, weekly or monthly basis depending upon the policies of the organisation.

The employee enters their name, clock number and department at the top of the time sheet together with details of the work carried out in the period and the hours spent on that work.

This enables the cost of each employee's labour hour to be correctly charged to the correct production cost centre.

2.8 Job sheets

Definition A **job sheet** records the number of each type of product that an employee has produced in the period.

Time sheets are prepared by employees who are paid for the number of hours that they work. However it is also possible to pay employees on the basis of the number of units of a product they produce, known as a results or **piece rate basis**.

For an employee paid on the basis of the number of products produced a time sheet is of little use. Instead, such an employee would complete some form of job sheet, which is used to calculate their gross pay.

Payment to the employee will then be based upon the information on this job sheet.

Conclusion   In order to correctly charge each cost centre for labour costs and calculate the correct amount of gross pay it is vital that the labour cost documentation is accurately completed.

3   Calculating gross pay – time related pay

There are two main methods of calculating the gross pay of employees:

- pay employees either for the time spent at work (**time related pay**)

- pay employees for the work actually produced, (**output related pay**).

3.1   Time related pay

Employees paid under a time related pay method are paid for the hours that they spend at work regardless of the amount of production or output that they achieve in that time. Time related pay employees can be split into two types, **salaried employees** and **hourly rate employees**.

3.2   Salaried employees

Definition   A **salaried employee** is one whose gross pay is agreed at a fixed amount for a period of time whatever hours that employee works in that period.

This might be expressed as an annual salary such as £18,000 per year or as a weekly rate such as £269.50 per week.

Each organisation will have a set number of hours that are expected to be worked each week, for example a standard working week of 37.5 hours, and salaried employees will be expected to work for at least this number of hours each week.

However if the salaried employee works for more than the standard number of hours for the week then the employment agreement may specify that overtime payments are to be made for the additional hours.

3.3   Hourly rate employees

Definition   An **hourly rate employee** is one who is paid a set hourly rate for each hour that he works.

These employees are paid for the actual number of hours of attendance in a period, usually a week. A rate of pay will be set for each hour of attendance.

3.4   Overtime

Definition   **Overtime** is the number of hours worked by an employee which is greater than the number of hours set by the organisation as the working week.

It is common that employees that work overtime are paid an additional amount per hour for those extra hours.

3.5 Overtime premium

Definition **Overtime premium** is the amount over and above the normal hourly rate that employees are paid for overtime hours.

Example

An employee's basic week is 40 hours at a rate of pay of £5 per hour. Overtime is paid at 'time and a half'.

The employee works a 45 hour week.

What is the total gross pay for this employee for the week?

	£
Bonus hours 40 × £5	200.00
Overtime 5 × £7.50	37.50
	237.50

Distinguish between the overtime payment and overtime premium for the week.

	£
Overtime payment 5 × £7.50	37.50
Overtime premium 5 × £2.50	12.50

4 Calculating gross pay – output related pay

Output related pay is also known as payment by results or piecework. This is a direct alternative to time related pay.

Definition Payment by results or piecework is where a fixed amount is paid per unit of output achieved irrespective of the time spent.

Activity 2 *(The answer is in the final chapter of this study text)*

If the amount paid to an employee is £3 per unit produced and that employee produces 80 units in a week how much would be his gross pay?

4.1 Advantages of payment by results

As far as an employee is concerned, payment by results means that they can earn whatever they wish within certain parameters. The harder they work and the more units they produce the higher the wage.

From the employer's point of view higher production or output can also be encouraged with a system of differential piecework.

4.2 Problems with payment by results

There are **two** main problems associated with payment by results. One is the problem of accurate recording of the actual output produced. The amount claimed to be produced determines the amount of pay and, therefore, is potentially open to abuse unless it can be adequately supervised. A system of job sheets and checking of job sheets needs to be in place.

UNIT 4 : SUPPLYING INFORMATION FOR MANAGEMENT CONTROL

The second problem is that of the maintenance of the quality of the work. If the employee is paid by the amount that is produced then the temptation might be to produce more units but of a lower quality.

For these reasons basic piecework systems are rare in practice – variations of these systems are used instead.

4.3 Piece rate with guarantee

A **piece rate with guarantee** gives the employee some security if the employer does not provide enough work in a particular period. The way that the system works is that if an employee's earnings for the amount of units produced in the period are lower than the guaranteed amount then the guaranteed amount is paid instead.

Activity 3 *(The answer is in the final chapter of this study text)*

Jones is paid £3.00 for every unit that he produces but he has a guaranteed wage of £28.00 per eight hour day. In a particular week he produces the following number of units:

Monday	12 units
Tuesday	14 units
Wednesday	9 units
Thursday	14 units
Friday	8 units

Calculate Jones's wage for this week.

4.4 Differential piece-work

Definition A **differential piece-work** system is where the piece rate increases as successive targets for a period are achieved and exceeded.

This will tend to encourage higher levels of production and acts as a form of bonus payment for employees who produce more units than the standard level.

Activity 4 *(The answer is in the final chapter of this study text)*

Payment by results rates for an organisation are as follows:

Up to 99 units per week	£1.25 per unit
100 to 119 units per week	£1.50 per unit
120 or more units per week	£1.75 per unit

If an employee produces 102 units in a week, how much will he be paid?

5 Bonus schemes

Bonuses may be paid to employees for a variety of reasons. An individual employee, a department, a division or the entire organisation may have performed particularly well and it is felt by the management that a bonus is due to some or all of the employees.

5.1 Basic principle of bonuses

The basic principle of a bonus payment is that the employee is rewarded for any additional income or savings in cost to the organisation. This may be, for example, because the employee has managed to save a certain amount of time on the production of a product or a number of products. This time saving will save the organisation money and the amount saved will tend to be split between the organisation and the employee on some agreed basis. The amount paid to the employee/employees is known as the **bonus**.

5.2 Method of payment

The typical bonus payable will often depend on the method of payment of the employee. The calculation and payment of bonuses will differ for salaried employees, employees paid by results and employees paid on a time rate basis.

6 Payroll

6.1 Initial recording of gross pay

The initial calculation and recording of gross pay for employees will be done in the payroll department. This department will then also calculate any PAYE and NIC and any further deductions in order to determine the net pay for each employee for the period.

6.2 Coding of labour costs

Payroll calculations are necessary in order to pay employees the correct amounts and to record the correct gross pay figure for financial accounting purposes.

However for cost accounting purposes more detail is needed. It is important that the gross pay of each employee is coded so that it is recognised by the correct production or service cost centre.

In some instances an employees clock card or time sheet might show that he worked for different cost centres during the period and therefore the gross pay must be broken down into the amount to be recognised by each cost centre and correctly coded as such.

6.3 Service cost centre employees

The employees of a manufacturing organisation do not all work for cost centres that actually produce the products. Many employees will work in service cost centres such as stores, the canteen, the accounts department and the sales division.

Costs need to be recognised by each of these service cost centres and therefore the gross pay of these employees must also be coded to show which cost centre they have worked for in the period.

6.4 Employers' National Insurance Contributions

When an employer pays the wages or salaries of an employee it must also pay a proportion of that amount to the Inland Revenue in the form of the Employer's National Insurance Contribution (NIC). This is a necessary cost of employing workers and is therefore part of the cost of labour for an employer.

6.5 Coding labour costs

The labour costs of the employees of an organisation will need to be coded to the appropriate cost centre but also coded according to the correct classification. The total labour cost of an employee can be made up of the following:

- Basic pay
- Overtime premium
- Bonus
- Employers' NIC

In many organisations only the basic pay for all hours worked in the period and the employers' NIC are treated as a labour cost. In contrast the overtime premium and any bonus payments are treated as expenses rather than labour costs. It is important to ensure that the person coding the labour costs has fully understood the organisation's policies on these matters.

6.6 Direct and indirect labour

Just as materials can be classified as direct or indirect so too can the labour costs depending upon the function of the employee.

Definition   **Direct** labour costs are the gross pay of the employees that work directly as part of the production process.

Definition   **Indirect** labour costs are the gross pay of employees that work in the organisation but are not directly involved with making the products.

In a manufacturing organisation therefore the factory workers who make the products would be direct labour whereas the factory supervisor would be an example of an indirect labour cost as although he is working in the factory he is not actually making any of the products.

7 Non-manufacturing organisations

Unit 4 does not concentrate solely on **manufacturing** organisations. It is also necessary to consider the costs that are incurred by **non-manufacturing** or service organisations.

7.1 Service industries

Many organisations do not produce a physical cost unit or product. Instead, they provide a service.

This might be an accountant that provides a tax service for clients or a transport organisation which transports goods for customers.

In exactly the same way as manufacturing organisations these service industries need to gather together their costs for information and control purposes.

7.2 Costs of service industries

Many service industries will not have large costs relating to materials, for example an accountancy firm.

Many service costs will be **labour based**, with all of the problems of overtime, holiday pay, bonuses etc involved in such costs.

Service industries will have many cost centres as in manufacturing organisations and relevant costs must be recognised for each cost centre.

7.3 Collection, classification and ascertainment of costs

Costs will be classified under appropriate headings for the particular service. This will involve the issue of suitable cost codes for the recording and collection of costs. For example, for a transport company, the main cost classification may be based on the following activities:

- operating and running the fleet
- repairs and maintenance
- fixed charges
- administration.

Within each of these there would need to be a sub-classification of costs, each with its own code, so that under vehicle fixed costs, there might appear the following breakdown:

- road fund licences
- insurances
- depreciation
- vehicle testing fees
- others.

The cost centres that might be in existence for such an organisation might be:

- maintenance department
- operating departments – may be sub-divided into:
  - different types of operations such as long-haul and short-haul types
  - vehicle fixed costs department
  - canteen
  - administration etc.

Conclusion In service industries the labour cost is often the major cost of the organisation. The gross labour cost, with all of its elements, must be recognised by the cost centres that have used each employee in just the same way as in a manufacturing organisation.

8 Expenses

The third type of costs are expenses.

Definition Expenses are all business costs that are not classified as materials or labour costs.

8.1 Types of expenses

An organisation will incur many different types of expenses. There may be expenses associated with the manufacturing process or the factory, the selling process, general administration or day-to-day running of the business and the financing of the business.

Manufacturing expenses – examples

Examples of expenses incurred during the manufacturing process are:

- sub-contractor's costs
- the power for the machinery
- the lighting and heating of the factory
- insurance of the machinery
- cleaning of the factory and machines

Selling expenses – examples

When selling goods to customers the expenses that might be incurred are:

- advertising costs
- costs of delivering the goods to the customer
- commission paid to salesmen
- costs of after sales care
- warehouse rental for storage of goods.

Administration expenses – examples

The everyday running of the organisation will involve many different expenses including the following:

- rent of buildings
- business rates on buildings
- insurance of the buildings
- telephone bills
- postage and fax costs
- computer costs
- stationery
- auditor's fees.

Finance expenses – examples

The costs of financing an organisation might include the following:

- loan interest
- lease charges if any equipment or buildings are leased rather than purchased.

9 Cost centres and expenses

9.1 Types of expenses

The various expenses of a business can be split into two types for our basic costing purposes. Those expenses that can be directly attributed to a **single cost centre** and those that need to split up among a **number of cost centres**.

9.2 Examples of directly attributable expenses

Examples of the expenses that can be directly attributed to a cost centre include the manufacturing costs (given above) which will be costs that must be recognised by the manufacturing cost centre and the selling costs (given above) that will be recognised by the sales department cost centre. This is the process of **allocation**.

9.3 Other expenses

If you look at the list of administration expenses (given above) you will realise that many of these relate to a number of different cost centres. For example, the rent of the buildings will relate to the manufacturing cost centre, the sales department cost centre, the accounting cost centre and the canteen cost centre. This applies equally to other expenses such as rates, insurance, electricity bills and telephone bills.

9.4 Apportionment of expenses

These joint expenses must therefore be split up in some equitable manner between each of the cost centres that incur some of these expenses. This process is known as **apportionment**.

9.5 Expense apportionment bases

In order to fairly apportion these expenses to cost centres, a suitable basis of allocation needs to be used. The organisation will have such bases set out in its policy manual and these must be used.

For example the **rent, rates and insurance** of the buildings may be apportioned to cost centres on the basis of the amount of **floor area** that each cost centre occupies. The **computer costs** might be apportioned on the basis of the **number of computer hours** that are used by each cost centre.

Example

Suppose that the rent, rates and buildings insurance for an organisation total £100,000. The floor space occupied by the five cost centres in the organisation is as follows:

	Square metres
Manufacturing cost centre	5,000
Stores cost centre	2,000
Canteen cost centre	1,500
Sales department cost centre	500
Administration cost centre	1,000
	10,000

Apportion the rent, rates and insurance expense to each cost centre on the basis of floor space occupied.

Solution

		£
Manufacturing	(£100,000 × 5,000/10,000)	50,000
Stores	(£100,000 × 2,000/10.000)	20,000
Canteen	(£100,000 × 1,500/10,000)	15,000
Sales	(£100,000 × 500/10,000)	5,000
Administration	(£100,000 × 1,000/10,000)	10,000
		100,000

9.6 Coding

In order to ensure that the correct amount of the allocated expenses are charged to each cost centre these allocations need to be carefully coded showing how much of the expense is to be recognised by each cost centre.

10 Quick quiz *(The answer is in the final chapter of this study text)*

1 What is the purpose of a purchase requisition?

2 What should the stores department check when goods are received?

3 What details should a purchase invoice be checked to before it is passed for payment?

4 What is the difference between overtime payment and overtime premium

5 How is the Employer's National Insurance Contribution normally coded in cost accounts?

6 How is the overtime premium normally coded in cost accounts?

7 Give an example of direct labour and indirect labour costs.

8 Give two examples of administrative expenses.

9 If an item of expense needs to be split between a number of cost centres what is the name of this process?

CHAPTER 4

The selling function

Focus

This chapter briefly outlines the duties of the sales function and its treatment as either a cost centre or a profit centre.

Contents

1 Making the sales
2 The sales function as a cost centre
3 The sales function as a profit centre
4 Classification and coding of sales invoices

Performance criteria

- Recognise appropriate cost centres and elements of costs (A – element 4.1)
- Extract income and expenditure details from the relevant sources (B – element 4.1)
- Code income and expenditure correctly (C – element 4.1)
- Refer any problems in obtaining the necessary information to the appropriate person (D – element 4.1)
- Identify and report errors to the appropriate person (E – element 4.1)

Key definitions	
Sales function	The area of the business dealing with sales which may be a cost centre or a profit centre
Coding listing	List of codes and code totals for each cost and income code of the business

1 Making the sales

Most organisations will have some form of **sales department** which will make the sales of the goods that have been manufactured or the services that the business provides.

1.1 Duties of the sales function

The sales function of an organisation will typically be responsible for the following:

- processing orders from customers
- negotiating the details of the order
- notifying the production department of the order details

- preparing the despatch note for the goods
- preparing the sales invoice
- organising any necessary advertising.

1.2 Make up of the sales function

In many organisations the sales may be made largely by telephone. A customer will telephone with an order and this will then be processed by sales department personnel and an order confirmation sent out to the customer.

In other cases the sales function may be made up largely of travelling salesmen who take orders personally from customers and then return the details to the sales department at head office for processing.

2 The sales function as a cost centre

Just as with any other area of the business that incurs costs, for cost accounting purposes the sales department may well be classified as a cost centre.

2.1 Costs of selling

The typical costs that might be incurred in the sales cost centre are labour costs and expenses.

2.2 Labour costs

The labour costs incurred will be the gross pay of all of the people who work in the sales department. This may be telephone sales personnel or travelling salesmen. The payroll should code the gross pay of each employee so that it can be recognised by the correct cost centre.

The gross pay of sales personnel may also include a particular type of bonus known as a sales commission. This may be based upon a fixed amount per order that is brought in by that sales person or it may be based upon a percentage of the value of each order.

2.3 Expenses – selling and distribution

The sales department will also incur a variety of expenses that must be recognised by the cost centre. These might include the following:

- **advertising costs** – these should be coded as selling costs when the invoice is received
- **transport expenses of delivering the goods to customers** – these will include petrol, insurance of the vehicles, etc
- **telephone costs** – a proportion of the organisation's telephone bill will be allocated to the sales cost centre
- **travelling expenses for the salesmen** – these might include petrol, insurance as well as any other incidental expenses such as overnight accommodation – all invoices and expense claims should be coded as costs for the sales cost centre.

3 The sales function as a profit centre

In some organisations the sales function may be treated as a profit centre rather a cost centre. This would mean that the income of the sales department would be the sales that are made and the costs would be the labour and expenses and probably also a cost for the value of the goods that are being sold.

3.1 Value of goods

If the sales function is to be treated as a profit centre then it is likely that it will effectively be charged with the cost of the goods that it is selling. This cost will be the total manufacturing cost of the goods, as determined by the management accountant, plus possibly a small profit element, or the purchase price, if finished goods are bought in.

3.2 Sales income

The income of the sales function will be derived from the sales value of the sales that it makes. This figure will be allocated to the sales profit centre by coding sales invoices not only to show the goods that have been sold and to which customer but also to indicate that the value of the invoice should be credited to the sales profit centre for costing purposes.

The sales figure that should be taken from the invoice is **after** any trade discounts but **before** adding any VAT. Remember that VAT is not part of sales income, it is simply a tax collected by the organisation on behalf of Customs and Excise.

Example

The sales function of an organisation has incurred the following costs taken from invoices and expense claims for the month of May:

	£
Advertising	2,400
Delivery costs	12,800
Salesmens' expenses	1,400

The gross pay of all the employees of the sales department for the month has been provided by the payroll department as £18,600 including sales commissions of £1,600.

The gross value of the sales including VAT at 17½% made by the department for the month is £176,250.

The management accountant has valued the goods that were sold at a total manufacturing cost of £50,000.

What profit has been made by the sales function for the month?

Solution

	£	£
Sales (net of VAT £176,250 × 100/117.5)		150,000
Costs:		
Cost of goods sold	50,000	
Labour cost	18,600	
Advertising	2,400	
Delivery costs	12,800	
Salesmens' expenses	1,400	
		85,200
Profit		64,800

4 Classification and coding of sales invoices

4.1 Coding

In many businesses the sales that are made will be of different types. This may be sales from different locations and/or sales of different types of products. As with costs these sales need to analysed and recorded to the correct profit centre and therefore the sales invoices must be correctly coded to the correct profit centre and as to the correct type of sale.

Example

Meredith Ltd is a company which sells DVDs, videos and CDs to a variety of retail outlets from three different locations, the Ladwell branch, the Opton branch and the Trinity branch. An extract from the coding policy for the company is given below. Each cost or income has the following coding:

First two digits denotes cost centre or profit centre

Next three digits denote the geographical location

Final two digits denote type of cost or income

01	Cost centre
02	Profit centre
100	Ladwell branch
101	Opton branch
102	Trinity branch
01	DVD sales
02	Video sales
03	CD sales

The sales invoice for the month up to 23 June have already been coded and included on the coding listing as follows:

Code	Month to date £	Week commencing 26 June £	Total for month £
0210001	7,346.78		
0210002	5,246.34		
0210003	2,583.45		
0210101	6,125.89		
0210102	4,126.40		
0210103	1,663.34		
0210201	3,672.49		
0210202	2,154.39		
0210203	1,236.73		

During the week commencing 26 June four further sales invoices were sent out. These invoices must be coded and the coding listing updated for the complete month.

INVOICE

MEREDITH LTD
Trading Park
Opton
OP3 4HG
To: Jones Suppliers

Invoice number: 235461
Date/tax point: 26 June 20X5
Order number: 146234
Account number: JO1

Quantity	Description	Unit amount £	Total £
120	CDs	4.99	598.80
85	DVDs	8.99	764.15
Net total			1,362.95
VAT			238.51
Invoice total			1,691.46

Terms Net 60 days

INVOICE

MEREDITH LTD
Retail Park
Trinity
TR5 9NF
To: My Music Ltd

Invoice number: 235462
Date/tax point: 27 June 20X5
Order number: 146241
Account number: MM2

Quantity	Description	Unit amount £	Total £
200	CDs	4.99	998.00
130	Videos	5.99	778.70
Net total			1,776.70
VAT			310.92
Invoice total			2,087.63

Terms Net 60 days

UNIT 4 : SUPPLYING INFORMATION FOR MANAGEMENT CONTROL

INVOICE

MEREDITH LTD
Retail Park
Trinity
TR5 9NF

Invoice number: 235463
Date/tax point: 29 June 20X5
Order number: 146244
Account number: HK1

To: HKL Entertainment

Quantity	Description	Unit amount £	Total £
140	DVDs	8.99	1,258.60
110	CDs	4.99	548.90
	Net total		1,807.50
	VAT		316.31
	Invoice total		2,123.81

Terms Net 60 days

INVOICE

MEREDITH LTD
Park Road
Ladwell
LD2 8GS

Invoice number: 235464
Date/tax point: 29 June 20X5
Order number: 146240
Account number: PC4

To: Picator Merchants

Quantity	Description	Unit amount £	Total £
160	DVDs	8.99	1,438.40
70	Videos	5.99	318.30
	Net total		1,857.70
	VAT		325.09
	Invoice total		2,182.79

Terms Net 60 days

Each of these invoices will now be coded to the correct profit centre and for the correct type of sale. Only the net amount is coded as the VAT is posted automatically.

Invoice coding

Invoice no:	235461	£598.80	0210103	
		£764.15	0210101	
Invoice no:	235462	£998.00	0210203	
		£778.70	0210202	
Invoice no:	235463	£1,258.60	0210201	
		£548.90	0210203	
Invoice no:	235464	£1,438.40	0210001	
		£419.30	0210002	

Now the coding listing can be updated and totalled for the month.

Code	Month to date £	Week commencing 26 June £	Total for month £
0210001	7,346.78	1,438.40	8,785.18
0210002	5,246.34	419.30	5,666.64
0210003	2,583.45		2,583.45
0210101	6,125.89	764.15	6,890.04
0210102	4,126.40		4,126.40
0210103	1,663.34	598.80	2,262.14
0210201	3,672.49	1,258.60	4,931.09
0210202	2,154.39	778.70	2,933.09
0210203	1,236.73	1,546.90	2,783.63

4.2 Summarising sales information by location

Once the sales invoices have been coded and included within the correct profit centre then it would be possible to summarise the information about the sales for a particular period. For example the sales for each location might need to be summarised for the month or the total sales of each type of product. This may mean that the codes given on a coding listing may have to be interpreted to determine which location or type of sale they relate to.

Example

Continuing with the previous example the updated coding listing is shown again:

Code	Month to date £	Week commencing 26 June £	Total for month £
0210001	7,346.78	1,438.40	8,785.18
0210002	5,246.34	419.30	5,666.64
0210003	2,583.45		2,583.45
0210101	6,125.89	764.15	6,890.04
0210102	4,126.40		4,126.40
0210103	1,663.34	598.80	2,262.14
0210201	3,672.49	1,258.60	4,931.09
0210202	2,154.39	778.70	2,933.09
0210203	1,236.73	1,546.90	2,783.63

You are now required to summarise the total sales for the month for each retail outlet. This can be done by totalling the figures for each relevant code. For example the Ladwell branch sales are codes 0210001, 0210002 and 0210003 which total to £17,035.16. This information could be presented as follows:

Actual sales by location - month of June

	£
Ladwell	17,035.16
Opton	13,278.58
Trinity	10,647.81
Total sales	40,961.55

4.3 Summarising sales information by product

Alternatively the management of the organisation may be interested in total sales across all branches but analysed by product.

Example

Continuing with the example of Meredith Ltd in order to find the total of sales by product again the codes must be considered carefully. For example all sales of DVDs end in the code 01 therefore the codes to be totalled to find the total DVD sales are:

	£
0210001	8,785.18
0210101	6,890.04
0210201	4,931.09
	20,606.31

This will be done for the other two products and the report can then be produced:

Actual sales by product - month of June

	£
DVDs	8,785.18
Videos	20,606.31
CDs	12,726.13
Total sales	7,629.11
	40,961.55

5 Quick quiz (The answer is in the final chapter of this study text)

1 Give three examples of duties of the selling function.

2 Give three examples of selling and distribution expenses.

6 Summary

The sales function of an organisation incurs costs like any other department of the organisation. However it also earns income in the form of the sales that are made, therefore it may be treated as a cost centre or alternatively as a profit centre. The sales invoices, as with costs, must be correctly analysed and coded.

CHAPTER 5

Comparison of information

Focus

In this chapter we will be dealing with comparisons of current actual costs with information from different sources. We must consider where the information for comparison comes from and how to make meaningful comparisons.

Contents

1 Comparisons required
2 Current period figures
3 Previous periods, corresponding periods and forecasts
4 Confidentiality

Performance criteria

- Clarify information requirements with the appropriate person *(A – element 4.2)*
- Compare information extracted from a particular source with actual results *(B – element 4.2)*
- Identify discrepancies *(C – element 4.2)*
- Following organisational requirements for confidentiality strictly *(E – element 4.2)*

Key definitions	
Previous period	The month or quarter prior to the current month or quarter
Corresponding period	The same month or quarter but for the previous year
Budget	Forecast figures for costs and income for a period
Flexed budget	Budget figures which are adjusted to reflect the actual level of activity for comparative purposes
Adverse variance	Where actual cost is higher than budgeted cost
Favourable variance	Where actual cost is lower than budgeted cost
Work in progress control account	Where all costs of production are recorded

1 Comparisons required

1.1 Previous periods

In some cases you will be required to compare current costs and income to the same costs and income from previous periods in order to determine any significant differences. The previous period's costs and income will have been summarised in management cost reports and you need to be able to find these reports in your organisation's filing system.

1.2 Corresponding periods

In some businesses the income and costs tend to be seasonal and therefore a comparison of one period to another will not be particularly meaningful. For example in a retail business the period just before Christmas may be unusually busy therefore a comparison of income between December and November may not give any useful information. However in such cases it may be more useful to compare one period to the corresponding period of the previous year. In the case of the retailer the figures for December could usefully be compared to those of the previous December.

Another way in which comparisons can usefully be made with a corresponding period is by comparing the year to date costs or income to the same cumulative period in the previous year.

Again the figures for the historic information should be available from past management cost reports which will be kept in the filing system.

1.3 Budgets

You may also be required to compare current costs and income to the amounts that were budgeted for this period. Again you will need to be able to find the relevant budgets in the organisation's filing system.

2 Current period figures

In order to carry out the required comparison it will be necessary to find the correct current figures. These may be found from management reports such as coding listings or from the cost bookkeeping ledger accounts.

2.1 Coding listings

The coding listings are the all of the costs or income for a period which have been allocated to each cost centre or profit centre. In some cases the coding listing may need to be updated to take account of the most recent figures before they can be used for comparison.

Example

Given below is a summary of the expenses incurred by cost centres for a business for the final week of September:

	£
021113	1,241
021114	883
021115	1,235
022113	512
022114	463
022115	987

You are also given the opening balances on the cost centre accounts which is the year to date apart from the last week in September:

Code	Year to date £	Update £	Closing balance at 30 September £
021113	31,236		
021114	145,346		
021115	23,875		
022113	65,489		
022114	7,235		
022115	12,345		

You will now need to update the opening figures in order to find the current year to date figures to use for comparison.

Code	Year to date £	Update £	Closing balance at 30 September £
021113	31,236	1,241	32,477
021114	145,346	883	146,229
021115	23,875	1,235	25,110
022113	65,489	512	66,001
022114	7,235	463	7,698
022115	12,345	987	13,332

2.2 Ledger accounts

It is also possible that you may have to extract figures for materials costs, labour costs or expenses from ledger accounts in the cost accounting ledger records. Therefore you will need an outline understanding of how these figures are recorded in the cost accounting ledgers.

2.3 Materials accounting

When materials are purchased by the business they are recorded as a debit entry in the materials control account. When materials are issued to production, via a materials requisition, they are credited to the materials account and debited to the work in progress control account.

Example

During the month of May £100,000 of materials were purchased but only £90,000 of materials were issued to the production process.

Materials controls account

	£		£
Purchases	100,000	Work in progress	90,000

Work in progress control account

	£		£
Materials control account	90,000		

Therefore if the amount of materials used for production in the month were required for comparison this could be found by locating the debit entry in the work in progress control account.

2.4 Accounting for labour costs

As with the materials cost the production labour cost for the period will be entered as a debit entry in the work in progress control account. However this figures comes from the gross wages control which will initially record the total wages cost.

Example

The business incurs £60,000 of wages costs for the month of which £45,000 were paid to production staff and £15,000 to general administration staff.

Gross wages control account

	£		£
Total gross wages	60,000	Work in progress	45,000
		Administration costs	15,000

Work in progress control account

	£		£
Materials control account	90,000		
Gross wages control	45,000		

The total wages from the gross wages control account are split between those relating to production which are debited to the work in progress account and those relating to other areas of the business, such as administration labour costs, are kept separate.

If the manufacturing labour cost for the month is required then this can be found either from the credit entry in the gross wages control account or the debit entry in the work in progress account.

2.5 Accounting for expenses

As with materials and labour costs any expenses that are directly related to production are gathered together in the work in progress control account.

Example

The business incurs £10,000 of production expenses and £6,000 of administration expenses during the month.

Expenses control account

	£		£
Expenses incurred	16,000	Work in progress	10,000
		Administration expenses	6,000

Work in progress control account

	£		£
Materials control account	90,000		
Gross wages control	45,000		
Expenses	10,000		

2.6 Comparisons

Now that we have determined how to gather both the historic and the current information it is now possible to consider how to make useful comparisons.

3 Previous periods, corresponding periods and forecasts

3.1 Comparison of information

There are many ways in which you might be requested to compare current costs and income to previous and corresponding control periods. In this section some typical examples will be considered.

COMPARISON OF INFORMATION : CHAPTER 5

It is always important to ensure that you understand precisely what is required of you as this comparison is likely to be a time consuming process and you do not want to waste time extracting information that is not required. Therefore if you have any doubts about precisely what information is required then always check with the appropriate person.

Example

Your organisation operates its sales function in three divisions, A, B and C and records sales separately for each division. You have been asked to compare this months sales (June) to those of the previous month. You have found the May information from the management accounting filing system and they are as follows:

	£
Division A	113,000
Division B	258,000
Division C	142,000

You have also found the sales ledger accounts for June which are as follows:

Sales account – Division A

	£		£
		Sales June	129,000

Sales account – Division B

	£		£
Sales returns June	15,000	Sales June	250,000

Sales account – Division C

	£		£
		Sales June	120,000

You are required to compare the sales for June to those for the month of May in a suitable manner.

Probably the simplest method of comparing this information would be in the form of a table showing the sales for each division and in total for each month. Care should be taken with Division B's sales and the returns must be deducted from the sales figure therefore a net sales balance should be found on that account as follows:

Sales account – Division B

	£		£
Sales returns June	15,000	Sales June	250,000
Balance c/d	235,000		
	250,000		250,000

FTC FOULKS LYNCH

Now a simple table can be prepared:

Divisional sales for May and June

	May £	June £	Increase/(decrease) £
Division A	113,000	129,000	16,000
Division B	258,000	235,000	(23,000)
Division C	142,000	120,000	(22,000)
Total	513,000	484,000	(29,000)

It might also be useful to include a further column to show the percentage increase or decrease in sales. The percentage change would be calculated as a percentage of the May sales as follows:

Division A $\quad \dfrac{16,000}{113,000} \times 100 = 14.2\%$

Division B $\quad \dfrac{(23,000)}{258,000} \times 100 = (8.9\%)$

Division C $\quad \dfrac{(22,000)}{142,000} \times 100 = (15.5\%)$

Total $\quad \dfrac{(29,000)}{513,000} \times 100 = (5.7\%)$

The table would then appear as follows:

Divisional sales for May and June

	May £	June £	Increase/(decrease) £	Increase/(decrease) %
Division A	113,000	129,000	16,000	14.2
Division B	258,000	235,000	(23,000)	(8.9)
Division C	142,000	120,000	(22,000)	(15.5)
Total	513,000	484,000	(29,000)	(5.7)

Activity 1 *(The answer is in the final chapter of this study text)*

You have been asked to compare the month 2 labour cost from last year to the month 2 labour cost for this year.

From the filed management accounts for last year you discover that the month 2 labour cost was broken down as follows:

	£
Production labour cost	336,000
Selling department labour cost	248,000
Administration department labour cost	100,000

The wages expense account for month 2 of this year is as follows:

Wages expense account

	£		£
Gross wages cost	990,000	Work-in-progress account	510,000
		Selling costs account	350,000
		Administration costs account	130,000

You are required to compare the labour costs for month 2 of the current period and the corresponding period.

3.2 Comparison to corresponding period

Rather than comparing figures from one month to the next or one quarter to the next it might be more useful to management to compare the figures for a particular period this year to the same period the previous year and determine any increases or decreases.

Example

In an earlier example we were given the total costs for the year to date as at 30 September for a variety of cost codes as follows:

Code	Year to date at 30 September 20X4 £
021113	32,477
021114	146,229
021115	25,110
022113	66,001
022114	7,698
022115	13,332

The current year is 20X5 and you now find in the management accounting records the figures for the same cost codes in the year to date to 30 September 20X4. Comparison can then be made:

Code	Year to date at 30 September 20X4 £	Year to date at 30 September 20X5 £	Increase/ decrease £
021113	30,551	32,477	1,926
021114	151,345	146,229	(5,116)
021115	26,790	25,110	(1,680)
022113	73,465	66,001	(7,464)
022114	6,124	7,698	1,574
022115	11,531	13,332	1,801
	299,806	290,847	(8,959)

3.3 Comparison to budgeted figures

Comparison might also be required between forecast or budgeted figures for a period and the actual results of the period. Upon comparing actual costs to budgeted costs, there may be a difference or discrepancy between them, known as the variance. If the actual cost is greater than the budget, this is adverse but if actual cost is less than budget, this is a favourable variance.

Example

You have been asked to prepare a comparison of the budgeted cost of materials and labour for production in week 17 to the actual cost for the week.

The budgeted costs were found in the filing system and it was discovered that they were as follows:

	£
Material X	117,000
Material Y	270,000
Labour	226,000

The actual costs for the period are as follows:

Stores ledger card

MATERIAL DESCRIPTION	Material X								
Code	M100								
	Receipts			Issues			Balance		
Date	Quantity	Unit price £	Total £	Quantity	Unit price £	Total £	Quantity	Unit price £	Total £
Bal b/f							10,000	15.00	150,000
Week 17				8,000	15.00	120,000	2,000	15.00	30,000

MATERIAL DESCRIPTION	Material Y								
Code	M101								
	Receipts			Issues			Balance		
Date	Quantity	Unit price £	Total £	Quantity	Unit price £	Total £	Quantity	Unit price £	Total £
Bal b/f							130,000	2.50	325,000
Week 17				100,000	2.50	250,000	30,000	2.50	75,000

Wages expense account

	£		£
Gross wages	470,000	Production costs	230,000
		Selling costs	110,000
		Administration costs	130,000

You are required to prepare a comparison of the budgeted and actual figures for week 17.

Costs – week 17

	Budget year £	Actual £	Variance £
Material X	117,000	120,000	3,000 adverse
Material Y	270,000	250,000	20,000 favourable
Labour	226,000	230,000	4,000 adverse

Note how variances can be either favourable or adverse depending upon whether the actual cost is smaller or larger than the budget cost.

Activity 2 *(The answer is in the final chapter of this study text)*

The budgeted costs for expected production of 100,000 units last week are given below:

	£
Labour	45,000
Materials	60,000
Production expenses	17,000

The actual costs were:

	£
Labour	42,000
Materials	62,000
Production expenses	16,000

You are required to compare budgeted costs to actual costs.

3.4 Sales and variances

Budgeted levels of sales can also be compared to actual sales and variances can be calculated. However some care should be taken with determining whether the sales variances are favourable or adverse. If actual sales are higher than budgeted sales then this is a favourable variance. Whereas if actual sales are lower than the budgeted sales then this is an adverse variance.

Example

Given below are the budgeted and actual sales for three products for the month of July and their variances. Make sure that you are happy with whether the variance is favourable or adverse.

Product	Budgeted sales £	Actual £	Variance £
Material X	117,000	120,000	3,000 adverse
X	450,000	430,000	20,000 adverse
Y	500,000	530,000	30,000 favourable
Z	410,000	400,000	10,000 adverse

3.5 Investigation of variances

Variances are of interest to management as they form part of the management process of control and managers will often need to investigate the cause of any variances. However in many organisations not all variances will be investigated only those that significant. Therefore you might be asked to prepare calculations showing each variance as a percentage of the budgeted figure indicating which are most significant and may deserve investigating.

Example

Given below are the actual costs and budgeted costs for a manufacturing process for the month of March:

Cost	Budget £	Actual £
Material X	100,000	105,600
Material Y	80,000	77,300
Labour	140,000	138,700
Expenses	60,000	67,400

We can now calculate the variances for each expense together with the percentage that each variance is of the original budgeted figure.

Cost	Budget £	Actual £	Variance £	Percentage
Material X	100,000	105,600	5,600 adverse	5.6% adverse
Material Y	80,000	77,300	2,700 favourable	3.4% favourable
Labour	140,000	138,700	1,300 favourable	0.9% favourable
Expenses	60,000	67,400	7,400 adverse	12.3% adverse

If the business has a policy of only investigating variances that are more than 10% of the budgeted figure then in this case only the expenses variance needs to be highlighted for investigation to management.

4 Confidentiality

4.1 Introduction

As part of the accounting team you will often find that you have access to documents and information about the organisation that other employees do not have. It is extremely important that you are always discreet and strictly follow all the confidentiality guidelines of your organisation.

4.2 Sales information

When dealing with sales invoices and credit customers it is likely that you may come across information regarding customers' credit ratings and financial position. Such information should never be disclosed.

4.3 Materials and expenses

When dealing with materials costs and expense details there may be many confidential areas that you come across, from suppliers details to sales representatives' expense claims.

4.4 Labour costs

Perhaps most importantly, when dealing with labour costs you may become aware of many personal details about employees within the organisation. Such information should always be treated with the greatest degree of confidentiality.

5 Quick quiz *(The answer is in the final chapter of this study text)*

1   Why might comparison to a corresponding period be more useful than comparison to a previous period?

2   What are the accounting entries for materials used in production?

3   If an actual cost is less than the budgeted cost is this a favourable or an adverse variance?

4   If actual sales income is less than budgeted sales income is this a favourable or an adverse variance?

6 Summary

This chapter has focused on the comparison of actual costs or income to previous or corresponding figures or budgeted figures. In order to do this the actual costs or income must be extracted from the management accounting information. When comparing the actual figures to previous periods or budgets it is important that comparison is "like for like" by using the principle of flexing costs or income for the actual level of activity.

CHAPTER 6

Reporting

Focus

This chapter deals with the most common methods of reporting the types of comparisons you may be asked to make.

Contents

1. Methods of reporting
2. A note
3. A letter
4. Electronic mail
5. Memoranda
6. Report writing

Knowledge and understanding

- Handling confidential information *(Item 9)*

- The organisation's confidentiality requirements *(Item 17)*

- House style for presentation of different types of documents, including word-processing documents *(Item 18)*

Performance criteria

- Provide comparisons to the appropriate person in the required format *(D – element 4.2)*

- Follow organisational requirements for confidentiality strictly *(E – element 4.2)*

Key definitions	
Letter	A document normally sent to a party external to the business
E-mail	Electronic form of communication either internally or externally
Memorandum	A relatively informal method of communication within a business
Report	A formal method of communication normally within a business

1 Method of reporting

In the previous chapter methods of comparing information were considered. When requested for such a comparison of information it will normally be requested in a particular format. This can range from an informal note through to a formal report. In this chapter we will consider each of the different methods of reporting.

1.1 House style

Although the basic requirements of each method of reporting will be covered in this chapter it is important to realise that each organisation will have its own style and methods of reporting. These will normally be contained in the organisation's policy manual and house styles should always be followed.

1.2 Confidentiality

It is extremely important that the information that has been requested is sent to the appropriate person and only that person and any others that you are specifically asked to send it to. Often the information is confidential and therefore should be treated with the highest respect and care.

2 A note

Probably the most simple and informal method of reporting information to another person in the organisation is by way of a note.

2.1 Format

There is no set format for a note although obviously it must be addressed to the appropriate person, be dated, be headed up correctly so that the recipient knows what it is about and include your name so that the recipient knows who it is from.

In most cases the information that you are reporting on will be important management information and therefore it is unlikely that a note would usually be the most appropriate format. Only use a note if specifically asked to by the person requesting the information.

3 A letter

A slightly more formal method of communicating information is in the form of a letter. However it would be quite unusual to communicate to another person in the same organisation in this way although a letter may be appropriate if the person to whom you are sending the information works in a separate location.

3.1 Format

A letter should always have a letter heading showing the organisation's name, address, telephone number etc. Most organisations will have pre-printed letterheads for you to use.

The letter must also be dated and the name and address of the recipient be included before the letter itself is started.

The method of signing a letter will depend upon the formality of the how the letter begins.

If a letter is started as 'Dear Sir' then the appropriate way to sign off the letter is 'Yours faithfully'.

However if the letter is started 'Dear Mr Smith' then the appropriate way to sign off the letter is 'Yours sincerely'.

4 Electronic mail

Most organisations are now fully computerised and most individuals within an organisation can communicate with each other via electronic mail or e-mail.

4.1 Format

A email must be addressed to the person to whom it is being sent using their email address. It should also be given a title so that the recipient can see at a glance who it is from and what it is about.

In terms of format of the content of the email then there are no rules other than any organisational procedures that should be followed.

5 Memoranda

Definition A memorandum (or memo) is a written communication between two persons within an organisation. The plural of memorandum is memoranda.

A memorandum serves a similar purpose to a letter. However the main difference is that letters are usually sent to persons outside the organisation, whereas memoranda or memos are for communication within the organisation itself. Memos can range from brief handwritten notes, to typed sets of instructions to a junior, to a more formal report to a superior. In general a memo can be used for any purpose where written communication is necessary within the organisation, provided this is according to the rules of the organisation.

5.1 Format

Many organisations will have pre-printed memo forms. In smaller organisations each individual may draft his own memoranda. However there are a number of key elements in any memorandum.

Memorandum

To:

From:

Date:

Ref:

Subject:

Body of memorandum

Signature:

cc:

Enc:

All memoranda will show who it is they are being sent to and from whom. The date and a suitable reference, for filing purposes, are also essential. The memorandum then must be given a heading to summarise its essential message.

The content of the body of the memorandum will be discussed in the following paragraph. Whether or not a memo is signed will depend upon the organisation's policy. Some organisations insist on a signature on a memorandum; others do not.

It is highly likely that a number of copies of memoranda will be sent out and these should be listed. Finally if there are any enclosures ie, additional pieces of information that are being sent out with the memorandum then these should be noted under this final heading of Enc.

5.2 Content of a memorandum

The details of the content and style of a memo will depend upon who is sending the memo, to whom they are sending it, the degree of formality required and the actual subject matter of the memo.

Some memos will simply be handwritten notes from one colleague to another.

If a memo is to be sent to a superior in the organisation, either showing information requested or making recommendations, then both the tone and the content might perhaps be slightly more formal.

Again if a manager is writing to junior personnel in his department his style may be of a more formal nature than if he were writing to another manager within the organisation.

Whatever the precise style and content of the memo some general rules apply:

- There should be a heading to give an indication of the subject matter.

- There should be an introductory paragraph setting the scene.

- The main paragraphs of the memo should follow in a logical order, so that the recipient clearly understands the arguments being put forward.

- There should be a summary of the main points.

6 Reports

Accountants are used to dealing with figures, but they must also learn to express themselves clearly in words. Accountants are (or should be) well prepared for the degree of precision and organisation required in report writing, but may need practice to improve their written style.

6.1 Format

The following guidelines for report writing should be observed.

(a) **Reporting objectives**

Every report has several objectives. Generally these will be to:

- define the problem

- consider the alternatives

- make a reasoned recommendation for a specific alternative.

(b) **Recipient**

The writer should consider the position of the recipient and design the report accordingly. Some recipients will require detailed calculations; others will have little time to study a lengthy report and should therefore be given one of minimum length consistent with providing the required information.

(c) **Heading**

Each report should be headed to show who it is from and to, the subject and the date.

(d) **Paragraph point system – each paragraph should make a point; each point should have a paragraph**

This simple rule should always be observed. Important points may be underlined.

(e) **Jargon and technical terms**

The use of jargon should be avoided at all times. If it is necessary to use technical terms, these should be fully explained, as should any techniques with which the recipient may be unfamiliar eg, decision trees, linear programming, marginal costing, etc.

(f) **Conclusion**

A report should always reach a conclusion. This should be clearly stated at the end of the report, not in the middle. The report should make it clear why you have arrived at the stated conclusion: it is not enough simply to state all the alternatives and then to recommend one of them without supportive reasoning.

(g) **Figures**

All detailed figures and calculations should be relegated to appendices, only the main results appearing in the body of the report. Remember that comparative figures will often be useful. The report should be made as visually stimulating as possible, for instance, by the use of graphs or charts instead of, or to supplement, figures.

7 Word-processed documents

All of the above documents would usually be produced using word processing software. Memos and short reports should follow your company style. An example report and memo follow.

REPORT

To: Managing Director

From: Candidate

Date: Dec 20X5

Subject: Net present value technique

The net present value technique relies on discounting relevant cashflows at an appropriate rate of return. It would be helpful to know:

1 Whether there are any additional cashflows beyond year five.

2 Whether the introduction of a new product will affect sales of the existing products E, C and R.

On the basis of the information provided, the project has a positive net present value of £28,600 and should be carried out.

> # INTERNAL MEMO
>
> **To:** Bobby Forster, Accounts Assistant
>
> **From:** General Manager
>
> **Date:** 28 October 20X4
>
> **Subject:** Budgeted production costs for 20X5
>
> As you know we have begun our budgetary planning exercise for 20X5
>
> I understand that you have been working on the analysis of budgeted production costs.
>
> Could you please pull together all the information you have gathered and carry out the allocation and apportionment exercise for production overhead costs for 20X5.
>
> Thanks. Then we will have the necessary information that we need to calculate the pre-determined overhead absorption rates for 20X5.

8 Quick quiz *(The answer is in the final chapter of this study text)*

1   List the key elements to be included on a memorandum.

9 Summary

For Unit 4 you are only required to provide relevant information to the appropriate person rather than draw any conclusions from that information. Therefore it is likely that the less formal methods of communication such as notes and memos will be more appropriate than a report.

CHAPTER 7

Spreadsheets

Focus

In this chapter you are guided through the basic techniques of producing a spreadsheet on the computer and basic word-processed documents.

Contents

1. Introduction
2. The use of spreadsheets
3. Accessing a spreadsheet
4. Moving around the spreadsheet
5. Entering data
6. Improving the spreadsheet's appearance
7. Word processed documents
8. Automatic corrections
9. Spell check

Knowledge and understanding

- Methods of analysing information in spreadsheets *(Item 7)*

- Methods of presenting information, including word-processed documents *(Item 8)*

- House style for presentation of different types of documents, including word processed documents *(Item 18)*

Key definitions	
Spreadsheet	A computerised table of rows and columns, forming cells into which numbers, text and formulae can be entered
Cells	Each box made by the horizontal and vertical lines of a spreadsheet
Formulae	The basic commands written into the spreadsheet

1 Introduction

For those unfamiliar with spreadsheet packages, this chapter will provide the basic introduction needed to feel confident to 'get into' Microsoft Excel and carry out simple information analysis tasks. This package has been chosen because it is the most popular and therefore the most likely to be used in your college or work environment. The editions and programs that you are using may not be the same as those used in this text. In that case, the screens you produce will not be identical to those shown here. However, all spreadsheet packages will perform the basic functions covered in this chapter and access to a different package will not cause too many problems.

If you are at all unsure, you should read the manual that accompanies your chosen spreadsheet.

2 The use of spreadsheets

2.1 What is a spreadsheet used for?

Much of the data of a company is likely to be held on a number of spreadsheets. They are a convenient way of setting up all sorts of charts, records and tables, including:

- profit and loss accounts
- sales forecasting
- budgeting charts
- breakeven point analysis
- mortgage payments
- stock valuation
- exchange rate charts.

Spreadsheets can be used for anything with a **rows and columns format**.

2.2 Spreadsheets

A spreadsheet is used to manipulate data. You could define it as a table of rows and columns that intersect to form cells. Each row is identified by a number and each column by a letter (or letters). Each cell has a unique identifier formed by a letter (or letters) and a number.

The word **spreadsheet** has its origins in the large sheets of paper used by accountants, over which they spread their figures and calculations in neat rows and columns. The little boxes made by the horizontal and vertical lines have their counterpart in the PC's spreadsheet and are called **cells**.

Into these cells may be entered numbers, text or a formula. A formula normally involves a mathematical calculation on the content of other cells, the result being inserted in the cell containing the formula. These are not visible when you are entering data but reside in the background.

Because most business worksheets are quite large, extending beyond the edge of the computer screen, the screen is in effect a 'window' into the worksheet. Some or all of the spreadsheet can be printed out directly or saved on disk for insertion into reports or other documents using a word processing package.

The power of spreadsheets is that the data held in any one cell can be made dependent on that held in other cells, so changing a value in one cell can set off a chain reaction of changes through other related cells. This allows 'what-if?' analysis to be quickly and easily carried out – eg 'what if sales are 10% lower than expected?'

3 Accessing a spreadsheet

3.1 Excel

In the instructions that follow you will be using the Excel for Windows (or similar) package to create a worksheet, make calculations, enter formulae and copy data.

The following should be read and attempted in full if you are unfamiliar with the use of spreadsheets. If you are confident using spreadsheets check through the notes and exercises for any areas you may not have covered previously.

If you do not have access to Excel it will be assumed that you can use a similar package and you should refer to your manual for the basic mouse clicks.

As you are introduced to more commands, the worksheet will provide more information and give you a way to make business forecasts, 'What if?' analysis. When you have completed your report, you will print out a copy to present to your manager.

3.2 Running the program

The way to gain access to the spreadsheet package depends upon the type of computer system in use. A **menu** may be available to allow access to the chosen software by entering a single number or letter or by use of a cursor or mouse.

If you are using the spreadsheet at work, you must check first with your supervisor that it is allowed and that you are using the right version of the software.

If you are working in a **Windows** environment, you will access the spreadsheet package using the mouse. Click on the Start button in the bottom left hand corner of the Window. Keeping the mouse button depressed move to highlight the 'Programs' and then to the package that you want to use. Click on the icon.

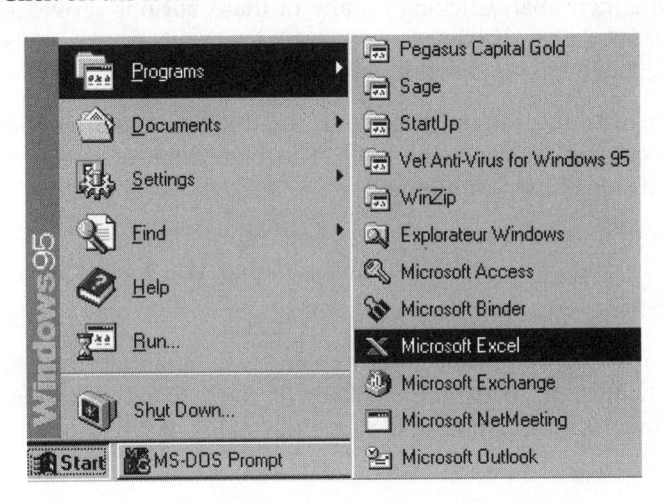

The opening screen in Microsoft Excel might look like this:

```
Title bar ──→  Microsoft Excel                              ─ □ ×  ←── Minimise/
Menu    ──→   File Edit View Insert Format Tools Data Window Help      Maximise/
Tool bar ──→                                                            Close
              Arial            ▼ 10  B I U  ≡ ≡  ▦ ▾ ♦ ▾ A ▾
                   A1          ▼     =                                ←── Formula
                                                                           bar/edit line
              Book1
                  A      B      C      D      E      F
Cell      ──→  1 Cell A1
pointer        2                              ←──────── Spreadsheet
               3
               4
               5
               6
               7
               8
               9
Status  ──→  Ready                                              NUM
bar
```

(Yours might look a little different if you have a different version of Excel)

On the screen you will see the **title bar**, the **menu bar, the function tool bar** and in the top right corner the buttons to **minimise, maximise**/restore and close the worksheet. As with most Windows programs you can change the size and move the Excel Window.

If your screen does not have a formula bar, a formatting bar or a toolbar you can show these by accessing **View** and then Toolbars from the menu at the top of the screen. You can then select (or deselect) what you want to show on the screen. A tick signifies that it is switched on.

The toolbars are below the menu bar. Clicking on any of these buttons provides a shortcut to selecting options from the menu bar. If you pause the pointer over a button a label will appear and, in the **status bar**, Excel will tell you what that button does.

The formula bar is between the spreadsheet and the toolbar. This provides you with information about the contents of the active cell. The co-ordinates of the active cell are displayed on the left-hand side of the formula bar.

The status bar is at the bottom of the screen. It gives you information about your spreadsheet, such as when you are opening or saving a file and whether you have CAPS LOCK, NUM LOCK or SCROLL LOCK on.

Scroll bars are used to move your spreadsheet both up and down and left to right. The vertical scroll bar (on the right hand side of the spreadsheet) is used to move up and down. The horizontal scroll bar (below the spreadsheet and above the status bar) is used to move left and right.

3.3 Vocabulary

The spreadsheet is now ready to go to work, but first you will need to know some basic terms and some spreadsheet vocabulary, so that you can give instructions.

- **Worksheet**: a worksheet or spreadsheet (as shown above) is the basis of all the work you do. It could be considered to be the electronic equivalent of an accountant's ledger.

- **Workbook**: is a collection of worksheets. The workbook is simply a folder that binds together your worksheets. When you open a new workbook, it automatically contains 16 worksheets.

- **Cells**: the worksheet is divided into columns and rows. The intersection of a column and a row is known as a 'cell'. To refer to a particular cell, use its column and row location. This is called a 'cell address', for example A1, B22, etc.

- **Columns**: each column is referenced by one or two letters in the column heading. The whole worksheet consists of 256 columns, labelled A through IV.

- **Rows**: each row is referenced by the row number shown in the row heading to the left of a row. There are 65,536 rows in Excel.

- **Sheet tabs**: these are between the worksheet and the status bar and are used to move between worksheets in your workbook.

- **Window**: you can only see part of the worksheet at any time; you could consider the screen to be a window onto the worksheet. You have the facility to move this window, so that you can view any part of the spreadsheet.

- **Cell pointer**: look at the cell that is highlighted; this highlighted area is known as the cell pointer. It indicates the cell in which you are currently working. The current cell location is also displayed on the edit line above the spreadsheet.

3.4 Creating and saving a new file

When you first open Excel, a blank spreadsheet appears on the screen and you can start typing straight away. At this point you can work on an established spreadsheet or start on a new one by creating a file as described below.

From the file menu choose the NEW option, and a new Excel workbook will appear on the screen. Once you have created a document, you must save it if you wish to use it in the future. To save a file:

- From the **FILE** menu choose the **SAVE AS** option.

- A dialogue box will appear.

- If necessary, use the DRIVE drop down menu to select the relevant drive; if you are saving to floppy disk, it is generally the 'a:' or 'b:' drive.

- In the **FILE NAME** text box type in the name you wish to use (up to 8 characters). All spreadsheet packages automatically add a three-digit extension to your filename. In Lotus it will begin with wk and in Excel it will begin with xl.

- Click on the **OK** button.

When you have saved a file once, you do not need to choose the **SAVE AS** option again, but simply choose **SAVE** from the **FILE** menu or click on the icon on the tool bar (picture of a floppy disk).

3.5 Closing a file/Quitting

When you have finished working on a spreadsheet and you have saved it, you will need to close it down. You can do this by either pressing the button at the top right hand side of the worksheet with a cross on it or by choosing the CLOSE or EXIT option from the FILE menu.

If you only want to exit Excel briefly and prefer not to close down the whole package you can switch to another application or back to the Windows Program Manager by pressing <Alt><Tab> repeatedly. This allows you to step through all the opened packages in rotation.

If you have changed the file, Excel will ask if you wish to save the changes you made before closing. Click on the appropriate button.

UNIT 4 : SUPPLYING INFORMATION FOR MANAGEMENT CONTROL

4 Moving around the spreadsheet

4.1 Cell pointer

The whole worksheet consists of many columns and rows. On opening the spreadsheet, you can only see a small part of it - generally columns A to H and rows 1 to 16. The screen is like a window onto the worksheet and you have the facility to move this window so that you can view any part of the worksheet. The cell pointer highlights the cell you are currently in.

By moving the cell pointer you are able to enter information into any cell of the worksheet. There are a number of ways of moving the cell pointer, but the easiest way is to use the mouse. You can move around the spreadsheet by positioning the **mouse pointer** over the appropriate cell and clicking to select that cell. If the cell address you want is outside the range shown in the current window, it is possible to move down or across the spreadsheet by clicking on the scroll bars to the side or below the Window. Alternatively, you can use the arrow keys on the keyboard.

4.2 Moving directly to a cell: the GOTO command

Sometimes we want to move to a specific address in the spreadsheet that is too far from our present position to warrant using the arrow keys to get there. On the top of the keyboard you can see a row of keys labelled F1 through to F12; these are known as 'function keys'. When these keys are pressed, a special function is invoked. For the moment we will explore the F5 key. This is the **GOTO key** in both Excel and Lotus 123.

Let us assume you wished to go to D19. Press F5 and a dialogue box appears. You are prompted to enter an address or range. Enter D19 and the cell pointer will go directly to cell D19.

Try moving around your worksheet now. You can find where the end is because the spreadsheet will beep whenever you attempt to go beyond the worksheet boundaries.

Activity 1 *(The answer is in the final chapter of this study text)*

What is the biggest co-ordinate in your worksheet?

4.3 The help facility

Excel has a comprehensive help facility, which provides both **general** help and **context sensitive** help.

To invoke the help command press the 'Help' button on the menu bar, the ? box on the toolbar or the shortcut key F1. To obtain information on any particular subject shown, move the mouse pointer over the required topic and click, or you may be prompted to type in a question.

Context sensitive help is available either when a help button is displayed in a dialogue box or when an error message is flashed onto the screen. Asking for help at this stage by either clicking on the help button, ? box or by pressing F1 will result in the help window appearing at the topic relevant to the problem encountered.

5 Entering data

5.1 Putting data onto the worksheet

Entering data on the worksheet is very easy. You simply type your entry at the keyboard, press return and whatever you typed will be placed in the current cell, ie where the cell pointer is.

As you type, each character will be displayed on the edit line at the top of the screen. The entry is not put onto the worksheet until you press the return key.

Move to cell A1. Type ABCDEF <Enter>

Now move to Cell A3. Type 123 <Enter>

When you have finished entering data you can either press the <Enter> key on the keyboard or click on the Enter Box (a green tick) on the formula bar.

If you change your mind about entering the data then either press the <Esc> key on the keyboard or click on the Cancel Box (a red cross) on the formula bar.

If you have made a mistake, you can press the 'backspace key' (the key above the ENTER key) to delete what you have done one character at a time. If you have already pressed the ENTER key, you can delete it by highlighting the cell or cells and pressing the Delete key.

There are three types of data that can be entered into your worksheet - text, numbers and formulae.

5.2 Entering text

Text is entered by simply typing into a cell. Typing any letter at the beginning of a cell entry causes it to be accepted as a 'label', rather than a 'value'. If the text you enter is longer than the width of the cell then the text will 'run over' into the next cell. But if the next cell also contains data/information then you will only see part of the text you entered, ie the label will be truncated.

There will be times when you want the spreadsheet to treat a number or a formula as text. To do this you must type an apostrophe in front of the number or formula you are entering, eg '01707 320903 or '=A4+D5.

5.3 Entering numbers

Numbers can be entered on the spreadsheet by simply typing into a cell. If the space in the cell is insufficient, the number will be shown in an exponential form on the spreadsheet, but the number will still be retained in full in the formula bar. If you want to see the contents of cells in full, the columns can be widened to accommodate the number (or text).

It is not necessary to put the commas in manually when entering large numbers (1,000 or more), because it is easy to format the data to display commas and decimal places to make the data easier to understand.

UNIT 4 : SUPPLYING INFORMATION FOR MANAGEMENT CONTROL

For example:

- Enter 123456 into a cell. Press Enter.

- Move the cursor back onto that cell, click on 'Format' in the menu bar, then 'Cells'.

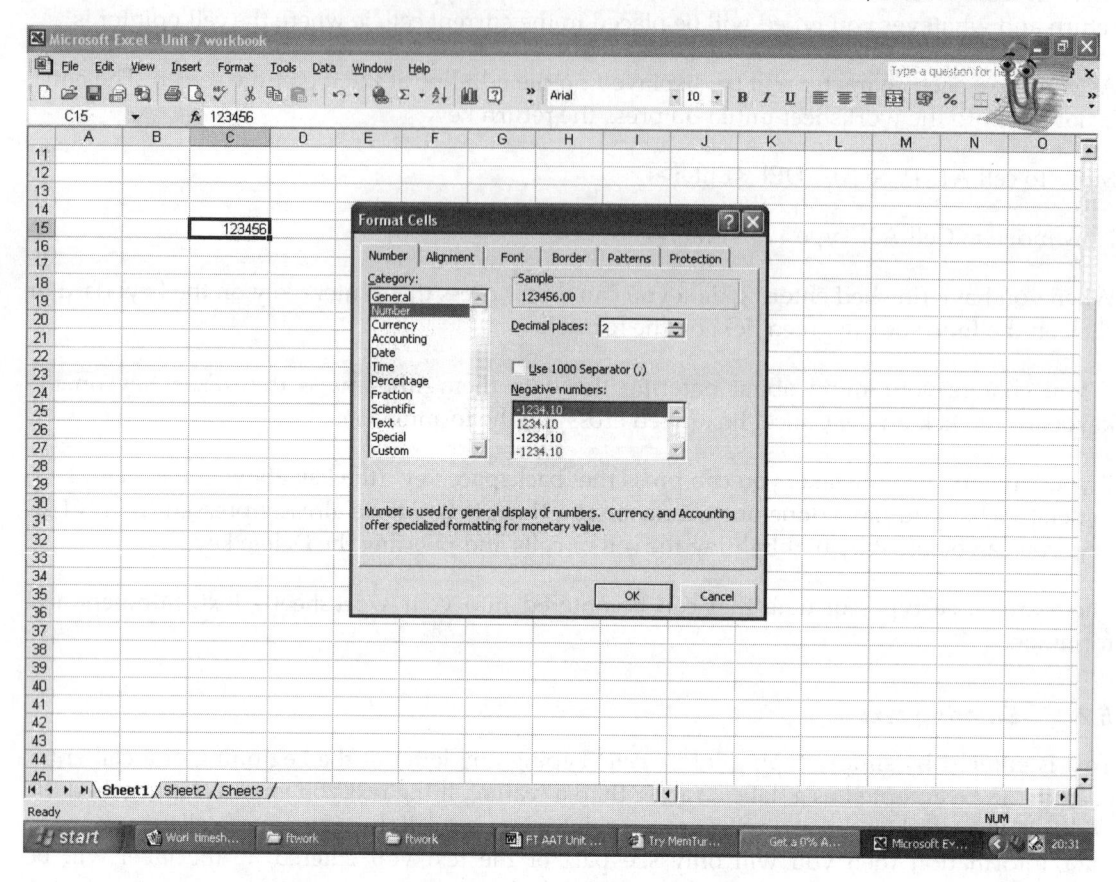

- Choose the 'Number' tab and then 'Number' from the category list.

- Now reduce the decimal places to '0' by clicking on the down arrow and tick the 'Use 1000 separator' box.

- Press OK. Your number should now be shown as 123,456

You can use the 'Currency' option from the category list to put £s in front – try it.

***

Activity 2 *(The answer is in the final chapter of this study text)*

We are to prepare a table to compare the results of three sales divisions. You are required to set up a spreadsheet for this comparison, with the appropriate headed columns and the basic input data, as shown below. In a later activity we shall complete this table by the use of formulae.

Divisional sales for May and June

	May	June	Increase/ decrease	Increase decrease
	£	£	£	%
Division A	113,000	129,000		
Division B	258,000	235,000		
Division C	142,000	120,000		
Total				

5.4 Entering formulae

The arithmetic operations and method of writing the basic formulae are very similar in all packages.

The **BODMAS (Brackets, Of, Division, Multiplication, Addition, Subtraction) rule** must be used to evaluate an arithmetic problem:

- Use brackets to clarify the correct order of operation and evaluate expressions within the brackets first.

- Calculate "of" expressions (eg 20% of the total).

- Perform division and multiplication before addition and subtraction.

- Work from left to right if the expression contains only addition and subtraction.

The basic commands for **statistical functions** that operate on lists of values are also very similar throughout the range of spreadsheet packages. Examples of these that you may use for this Unit are:

SUM   The sum of the values in list

AVG   The average of the values in list

A formula always starts with an equal sign (=) in Excel. If you start it with an equal sign (=) in Lotus 123, it automatically converts it to a plus (+) sign. Formulae consist of numbers, cell co-ordinates (eg A2, F7), operators and functions. Operators perform actions on numbers and co-ordinates. Examples of operators are plus, minus, divide and multiply. Functions perform more advanced actions on numbers and co-ordinates.

To enter a formula:

- Select the cell where you want to enter the formula.

- Press the equal sign (=) on the keyboard (or click on the sign in the formula bar, if one is shown).

- Key in the formula directly from the keyboard or use the mouse to select the cells you want in the formula. There are no spaces in a formula.

- Press the <Enter> key.

When you have entered a formula, the resulting value appears in that cell. The formula is only visible in the formula bar.

Typical formulae:

=(A6+C10)-E25 Adds A6 with C10 and subtracts E25

=(H19*A7)/3   Multiplies H19 with A7 and divides the total by 3

=SUM(L12:L14) A quick way of adding L12 + L13 + L14

An even quicker way to add a row or column of numbers is to click the button in the toolbar for Lotus 1-2-3. The equivalent button in MS Excel is the Greek symbol sigma.

5.5 What to do if you make a mistake

If you enter data incorrectly and you notice the error before pressing the return key then you can use the backspace key, which deletes characters from the entry, working from right to left. For example, let us assume that you wanted to enter the label 'Costs' into cell C1, but instead typed 'Cists'.

- Move cell pointer to C1
- Type   Cists (do not press the return key)
- Press backspace key five times
- Type   Costs
- Press the return key and 'Costs' will now appear in C1

Another method you can use if you notice the error before pressing Enter is to press the Esc key. The program will cancel what you have entered and return you to the Ready mode. You then simply re-key.

If you spot the error after you have pressed the **Enter** key then you could simply retype the entry, press **Enter** and the current contents of the cell will be replaced with this entry. For example, if you wished to change the contents of cell C1 from 'Costs' to read 'Total', simply re-key the entry.

- Ensure the cell pointer is still at C1
- Type   Total
- Total will now appear in C1

It would be frustrating if you had completed a long entry, spotted an error, and had to re-key the whole entry again. The spreadsheet comes to your aid with F2 - the **Edit** key.

Move the cell pointer to the cell containing the error, press F2. You will be put into **Edit** mode. The contents of the cell will be displayed on the edit bar with the cursor placed after the last character of the entry. (Alternatively you can put the cursor at the end of the contents displayed in the edit bar and click.) You may then use the following editing features.

- Arrow Left - will move the cursor one character to the left
- Arrow Right - will move the cursor one character to the right
- Home - will move the cursor to the first character of the entry
- End - will move the cursor to the last character of the entry

5.6 Exercise 1 - Basic data entry

In Excel, open a new blank worksheet and enter the following data. Leave plenty of space so that the titles are distinct. You will probably be putting the first invoice number in row 6.

Sales Invoices	August 20X0		
Invoice	Firm	Items	Price
1001	AB Plastics Ltd	10	0.2
1002	J Cables Ltd	21	0.2
1003	DC Covers Ltd	45	0.2
1004	DC Covers Ltd	42	0.2
1005	J Cables Ltd	500	0.2
1006	AB Plastics Ltd	25	0.2
1007	J Hoggs Ltd	300	0.2
1008	L Quick Ltd	1000	0.2
1009	DC Covers Ltd	50	0.2
1010	AB Plastics Ltd	12	0.2
1011	AB Plastics Ltd	15	0.2
1012	J Hoggs Ltd	350	0.2
1013	L Quick Ltd	1500	0.2
1014	J Hoggs Ltd	400	0.2
1015	L Quick Ltd	1250	0.2
1016	DC Covers Ltd	90	0.2
1017	F Browns Ltd	48	0.2
1018	L Quick Ltd	500	0.2
1019	F Browns Ltd	52	0.2
1020	F Browns Ltd	25	0.2

Don't worry if some of the columns don't seem wide enough - type in the whole name – we will adjust this later.

5.7 Adding basic formulae

Excel allows you to build up mathematical formulae to perform many useful functions, eg add up data, find average values, produce variances, add or subtract VAT, etc.

We will look at building up some basic formulae, which are commonly used in financial spreadsheets. In this exercise, we are going to calculate the Net price, the VAT and the Gross. You need to add three more columns after Price and label them: Net, VAT and Gross respectively.

(a) **Multiply** - in the 'Net' column we are going to put a formula to multiply the Items by the Price.

- Click on first entry in Net column (E6 probably)

- Type an = in the formula bar

- Click on first entry in the Items column (or type the address in - C6 probably)

- Type a * (to multiply)

- Click on first entry in the Price column (D6 probably)

- Press <Return> or OK

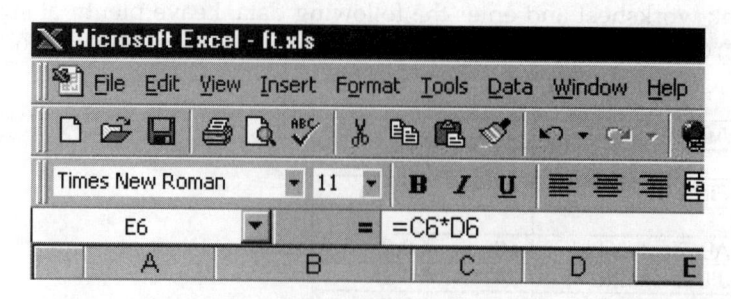

(b) Using the same type of multiply formula in the VAT column (F6 probably), calculate the VAT on the Net figure: this will be =E6*0.175.

(c) **Add** - we want to add the VAT to the Net to give us the Gross figure in G6

- Click on G6
- Type an = in the formula bar (or click on the = sign)
- Click on E6
- Type a +
- Click on F6
- Press <Return> or OK

(d) We have completed the first line of the schedule. Rather than individually repeating these operations for each of the remaining lines, we can simply copy the completed line into the remaining lines.

5.8 Copying

Shown below are the Cut, Copy and Paste buttons toolbar at the top of the screen on both Excel (left) and Lotus

(If you can't see all of these on your toolbar, click on the >> button, which will display more buttons.)

Cut then **paste** is used to **move** cells from one area of the spreadsheet to another.

Copy then **paste** is used to **copy** cells from one area to another.

Copying and pasting or cutting and pasting operations always have two parts:

- define the range you want to copy or cut **from**; then
- define the range that you want to copy or move **to**.
- So, for example, to put in '£' signs across the columns in your sales invoice schedule:
- Click on cell D5 and key in '£, press Enter. Go back to D5 and click on the button to place the text in the centre of the cell.

This is the range you want to copy from. (Here the range is a single cell.)

- Click the **copy** button on the toolbar (next to scissors). The border of D5 will start to shimmer.

- Position the cursor over cell D5, hold down the mouse button and drag to the right until cells D5 to G5 have been highlighted (D5 will be white, E5 to G5 will be black or blue). This is the range to copy to.

- Click on the **paste** button on the toolbar. The '£' sign has been copied from D5 and should now appear in E5 to G5.

You can copy formulae to different cells by the same method. Try to copy the formula from E6 into the range E7 to E25. Then from F6 to F7:F25 and G6 to G7:G25. Note that the cell references change automatically when formulae are copied.

Your spreadsheet should now look like this:

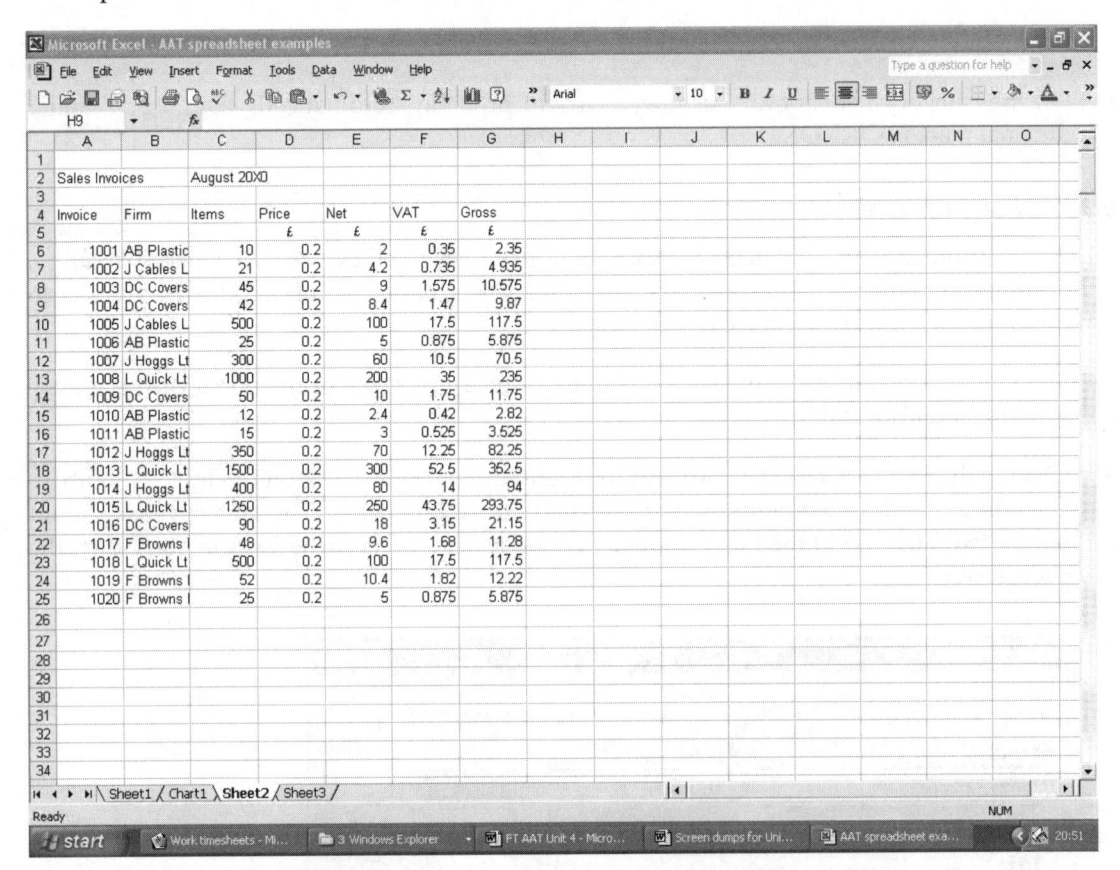

	A	B	C	D	E	F	G
1							
2	Sales Invoices		August 20X0				
3							
4	Invoice	Firm	Items	Price	Net	VAT	Gross
5				£	£	£	£
6	1001	AB Plastic	10	0.2	2	0.35	2.35
7	1002	J Cables L	21	0.2	4.2	0.735	4.935
8	1003	DC Covers	45	0.2	9	1.575	10.575
9	1004	DC Covers	42	0.2	8.4	1.47	9.87
10	1005	J Cables L	500	0.2	100	17.5	117.5
11	1006	AB Plastic	25	0.2	5	0.875	5.875
12	1007	J Hoggs Lt	300	0.2	60	10.5	70.5
13	1008	L Quick Lt	1000	0.2	200	35	235
14	1009	DC Covers	50	0.2	10	1.75	11.75
15	1010	AB Plastic	12	0.2	2.4	0.42	2.82
16	1011	AB Plastic	15	0.2	3	0.525	3.525
17	1012	J Hoggs Lt	350	0.2	70	12.25	82.25
18	1013	L Quick Lt	1500	0.2	300	52.5	352.5
19	1014	J Hoggs Lt	400	0.2	80	14	94
20	1015	L Quick Lt	1250	0.2	250	43.75	293.75
21	1016	DC Covers	90	0.2	18	3.15	21.15
22	1017	F Browns I	48	0.2	9.6	1.68	11.28
23	1018	L Quick Lt	500	0.2	100	17.5	117.5
24	1019	F Browns I	52	0.2	10.4	1.82	12.22
25	1020	F Browns I	25	0.2	5	0.875	5.875

6 Improving the spreadsheet's appearance

6.1 Finishing the spreadsheet

We are going to tidy up the spreadsheet and finish with the totals in row 27.

- In E27 we are going to total the column of values in cells E6 to E25.

- In E27 type =SUM(

- Click in E6 and look in the cell value bar. It should now read =SUM(E6

- Type ":" to indicate a range then click on cell E25 and type)

- Press <Return> or OK

The answer to the sum of the cell values should appear in cell E27 (1247). Label this row 'Total' in, say, B27.

All formulae can be entered by a combination of typing and using the pointer.

Note. A shortcut to summary values is to use the Σ symbol from the tool bar.

- Try this in columns F and G. In F27 click on Σ and press enter. Excel will automatically total the numbers in the cells above (you should get 218.225 and 1465.225 respectively).

6.2 Formatting numbers

To make your monetary data 100% clearer we need to format it to monetary amounts. For each of the columns with a '£' at the top (probably D, E, F and G):

- Highlight the column of figures to be formatted (eg E6 to £27).

- Click on 'Format' on the menu bar, then choose 'Cells'.

- On the category list choose 'Currency'. It will probably automatically assign a '£' and 2 decimal places. Click OK.

6.3 Formatting text

Making the spreadsheet look good is more than just a cosmetic exercise. Proper formatting, underlining and emboldening can make the spreadsheet easier to follow, draw attention to important figures and reduce the chance of errors.

To format the data you have entered and improve the appearance of the spreadsheet, we are going to do a number of things:

- Change the font to Times New Roman throughout. To do this click on the first cell with an entry in it and drag the mouse to the last cell with an entry in it. The area covered should be shaded. Then go to the Format menu and select Cells. Select the Font tab and then the chosen style.

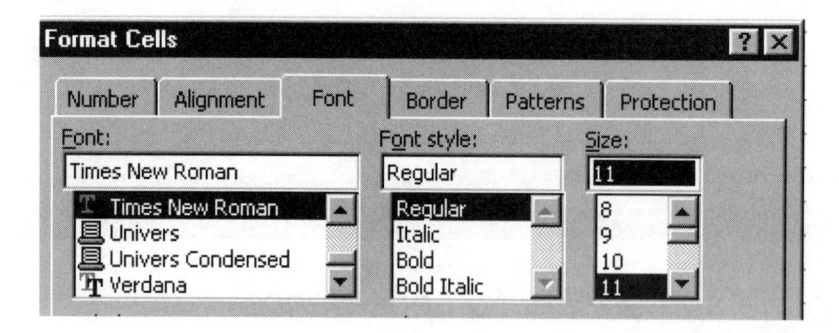

- The style format should be Times New Roman throughout with a font size of 14 for the titles and 11 for the main body of the text.

- Put the titles in bold. One way of doing this would be to activate the cells by clicking and dragging the cursor over them, then clicking on the **B** button (Bold) on the tool bar. Alternatively, all entries in a row or column can be selected by clicking on the letter at the head of the column or the number at the very left of the row.

- The Firm column B is not wide enough initially to enter the full details. Change the column width of B to 15 characters by placing the mouse pointer in the column heading at the intersection between column B and C. A two headed arrow should appear. Drag this to the right until the column is wide enough. Adjust the width of the other columns to accommodate the entries comfortably.

- Align the column headings. If you look at your spreadsheet so far you will see that all the text is left justified in the cells (moved as far as possible to the left) and the numbers are all right justified (moved to the right in each cell). To adjust this use the align buttons on the formatting toolbar (to the right of the underline U) – say, centre the Invoice numbers, Firm name and Items.

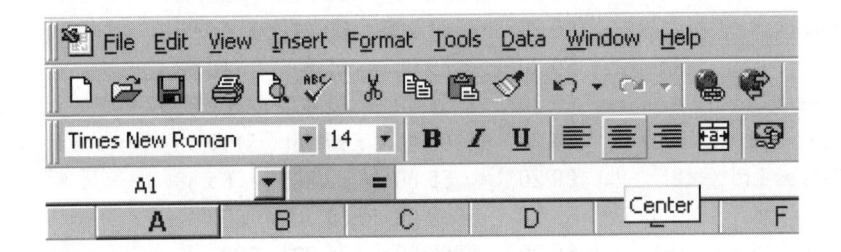

- Underline the totals by highlighting the cells containing the totals. Click on 'Format' on the menu bar, then click on 'Cells', then 'Border' tab, and a window similar to the following will appear.

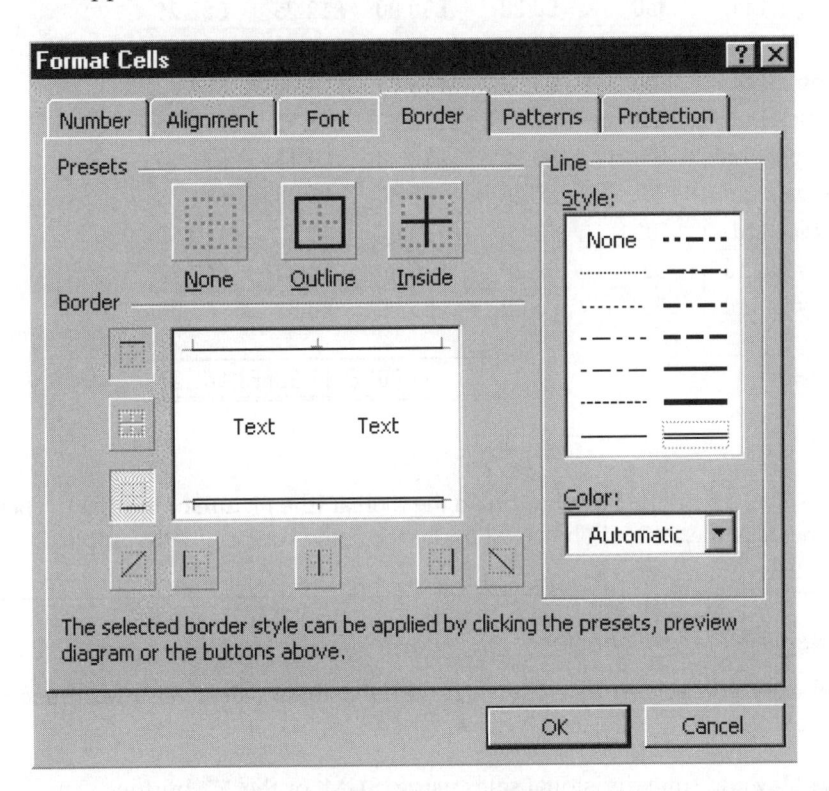

The box on the left shows the edges of the cell or selection of cells, which will have a border. The box on the right shows the types of lines that are available. Click on the top line on the left-hand list and then on the single, non-bold line (probably already selected) in the right hand options. The top of the 'totals' cells should now have a single underlining. Now click on the bottom line and then on the double under-lining style. Click on OK.

UNIT 4 : SUPPLYING INFORMATION FOR MANAGEMENT CONTROL

The finished spreadsheet should appear as follows:

	A	B	C	D	E	F	G
2	Sales Invoices		August 20X0				
3							
4	Invoice	Firm	Items	Price	Net	VAT	Gross
5				£	£	£	£
6	1001	AB Plastics Ltd	10	£0.20	£2.00	£0.35	£2.35
7	1002	J Cables Ltd	21	£0.20	£4.20	£0.74	£4.94
8	1003	DC Covers Ltd	45	£0.20	£9.00	£1.58	£10.58
9	1004	DC Covers Ltd	42	£0.20	£8.40	£1.47	£9.87
10	1005	J Cables Ltd	500	£0.20	£100.00	£17.50	£117.50
11	1006	AB Plastics Ltd	25	£0.20	£5.00	£0.88	£5.88
12	1007	J Hoggs Ltd	300	£0.20	£60.00	£10.50	£70.50
13	1008	L Quick Ltd	1000	£0.20	£200.00	£35.00	£235.00
14	1009	DC Covers Ltd	50	£0.20	£10.00	£1.75	£11.75
15	1010	AB Plastics Ltd	12	£0.20	£2.40	£0.42	£2.82
16	1011	AB Plastics Ltd	15	£0.20	£3.00	£0.53	£3.53
17	1012	J Hoggs Ltd	350	£0.20	£70.00	£12.25	£82.25
18	1013	L Quick Ltd	1500	£0.20	£300.00	£52.50	£352.50
19	1014	J Hoggs Ltd	400	£0.20	£80.00	£14.00	£94.00
20	1015	L Quick Ltd	1250	£0.20	£250.00	£43.75	£293.75
21	1016	DC Covers Ltd	90	£0.20	£18.00	£3.15	£21.15
22	1017	F Browns Ltd	48	£0.20	£9.60	£1.68	£11.28
23	1018	L Quick Ltd	500	£0.20	£100.00	£17.50	£117.50
24	1019	F Browns Ltd	52	£0.20	£10.40	£1.82	£12.22
25	1020	F Browns Ltd	25	£0.20	£5.00	£0.88	£5.88
26							
27		Total			£1,247.00	£218.23	£1,465.23
28							

Save your spreadsheet by clicking on the **Save** button on the toolbar (the picture of the disk). There is no need to enter a name this time, as it will be saved under the name you originally supplied.

Activity 3 *(The answer is in the final chapter of this study text)*

Go back to the spreadsheet you set up in Activity 2, for Divisional sales. Use formulae to complete the spreadsheet:

- Put in totals for the May and June divisional sales using 'SUM' or the $\sum$ button.

- Compute the absolute increase/decrease for each division, and in total, using '-'.

- Compute the percentage changes relative to May's sales to one dp.
  (Hint: compute change/May's sales, then use Format-Cell-Number-Percentage)

Finally, tidy up the presentation of your spreadsheet.

7 Word processed documents

7.1 Introduction

You need to be able to produce a word processed report. The purpose of this section is to introduce you to the basic techniques of word processing.

We are not attempting to provide you with a detailed course on word processing or the use of spreadsheets, that would take far too long and is not necessary for the requirements of the standards. All that is required is that you have reasonable typing skills and can deal with spreadsheets as covered elsewhere in this text.

Note: The following instructions are specifically relevant for *Word 2000*.

In order to illustrate the various changes we can make we are going to use the following sub-paragraph:

99.1 Illustrative paragraph

The quick brown fox jumped over the lazy dog. In order to get more exercise the quick brown fox did it several times. The quick brown fox jumped over the lazy dog. The quick brown fox jumped over the lazy dog. The quick brown fox jumped over the lazy dog. The quick brown fox jumped over the lazy dog.

7.2 Typeface

There are numerous typefaces that are available and any number of typefaces can be used within a document. For example you may want your main headings to be in one typeface with the body text be in another.

There are a number of ways to select a typeface but the easiest keyboard method is [Ctrl + Shift + F], then use your north and south cursor keys to select the typeface that you require. Remember to press [enter] once you have selected the typeface that you require.

Illustration

In order to illustrate this, we shall take the above illustrative paragraph which is currently in Book Antiqua and we shall convert it to Arial.

Step 1

Place the cursor before the first number of the heading of the illustrative paragraph above, hold down the Shift key and use the down arrow to highlight the paragraph.

Step 2

Click your mouse on the small down arrow next to the typeface box on the toolbar. This drops down a menu of typefaces. Use the scroll bar to move up and down the menu and click on the typeface you want (in this case Arial). The paragraph you have selected will now change to Arial.

You can have great fun converting the paragraph to some fairly extraordinary typefaces, but remember that you are doing this in the context of a business report and funny typefaces are unimpressive, often difficult to read and may well look unprofessional in this context.

7.3 Point size

Again you want may to differentiate text by making text larger or smaller. The method of doing this is similar to that described above, and we shall now illustrate how to convert the same paragraph as before to a 16 point, Arial typeface.

Step 1

Exactly as in step 1 above, highlight the Arial paragraph you produced.

Step 2

Click your mouse on the small down arrow next to the point size on the toolbar. A menu of point sizes will drop down. Click on the point size 16. The paragraph will immediately change to the larger 16 point typeface.

The result of 7.2 and 7.3 above will be to produce a paragraph looking as follows.

99.1 Illustrative paragraph

The quick brown fox jumped over the lazy dog. In order to get more exercise the quick brown fox did it several times. The quick brown fox jumped over the lazy dog. The quick brown fox jumped over the lazy dog. The quick brown fox jumped over the lazy dog.

7.4 Copying text

It is often very useful to be able to copy text from one place in a document to another. This is done as follows.

Step 1

Highlight the text to be copied as described above.

Step 2

Press [Ctrl + C]. Doing this effectively holds the paragraph in the computer's memory but there is no visible sign that anything has happened.

Step 3

Move the cursor to the new location where you want to copy the text and press [Ctrl + V]. The copied text will appear in the new location (and will still be in its original location).

7.5 Moving text

It is often very useful to be able to move text from one place in a document to another. This is done as follows.

Step 1

Highlight the text to be moved as described above.

Step 2

Press [Ctrl + X]. Doing this effectively holds the paragraph in the computer's memory and it will disappear from its original location.

Step 3

Move the cursor to the new location where you want to move the text and press [Ctrl + V]. The moved text will appear in the new location (and will no longer be in its original location).

7.6 Altering margins – 1

In order to change the appearance of your document, it is useful to be able to alter the margins and alignment of the left hand side of the text. You will notice that in this text book the left hand margin of the text is aligned underneath the first number of each numbered sub-paragraph. You may prefer to align the left hand side of the text with the first word of the numbered title. You may do this as follows.

Step 1

Highlight the text as above (excluding the numbered sub-title).

Step 2

Press [Ctrl + M]. The text of the paragraph will now shift to the right and align the left hand side under the words of the sub-heading as shown below.

> 99.1 **Illustrative paragraph**
> The quick brown fox jumped over the lazy dog. In order to get more exercise the quick brown fox did it several times. The quick brown fox jumped over the lazy dog. The quick brown fox jumped over the lazy dog. The quick brown fox jumped over the lazy dog. The quick brown fox jumped over the lazy dog.

In order to return the format of the text to its original, you do the following.

Step 1

Highlight the text to be realigned as above.

Step 2

Press [Ctrl + Shift + M]. The text will move back to the main margin as shown below.

> 99.1 **Illustrative paragraph**
> The quick brown fox jumped over the lazy dog. In order to get more exercise the quick brown fox did it several times. The quick brown fox jumped over the lazy dog. The quick brown fox jumped over the lazy dog. The quick brown fox jumped over the lazy dog.

7.7 Positioning of text

There are numerous ways that you can alter the alignment of your paragraphs. Below we briefly summarise the ways this can be done. The first step is always to highlight the text. The second step will depend on what effect you are trying to achieve and these are summarised below. We suggest that you experiment with these to become familiar with the sorts of effects you can achieve.

- [Ctrl + E] enables you to centralise text.

- [Ctrl + J] enables you to justify the text to the left and right. This means that the computer will automatically work out the correct length of each line so that both the left and right margins are perfectly aligned.

- [Ctrl + R] enables you to justify text to the right. In this case only the right hand margin is aligned.

- [Ctrl + L] enables you to justify text to the left. In this case only the left hand margin is aligned.

- [Ctrl + T] enables you to start your text at the left hand margin with all subsequent lines of text aligned to the tab position (this is referred to as a hanging indent).

- [Ctrl + Shift + T] returns the second line of text to the main margin.

8 Automatic corrections

Word contains an automatic correction feature *AutoCorrect* that automatically detects and corrects typographical errors, mis-spelled words, incorrect capitalisation and so on. You may however find that some of the options hinder rather than helps you! An example is where *AutoCorrect* changes (c) to ©.

To display the automatic correction feature press [Alt + T], then press [A].

A window will appear offering numerous alternative autocorrect features. Most of them are fairly obvious and you should experiment in a document especially created for the purpose – not one that contains important information that you would not want to lose.

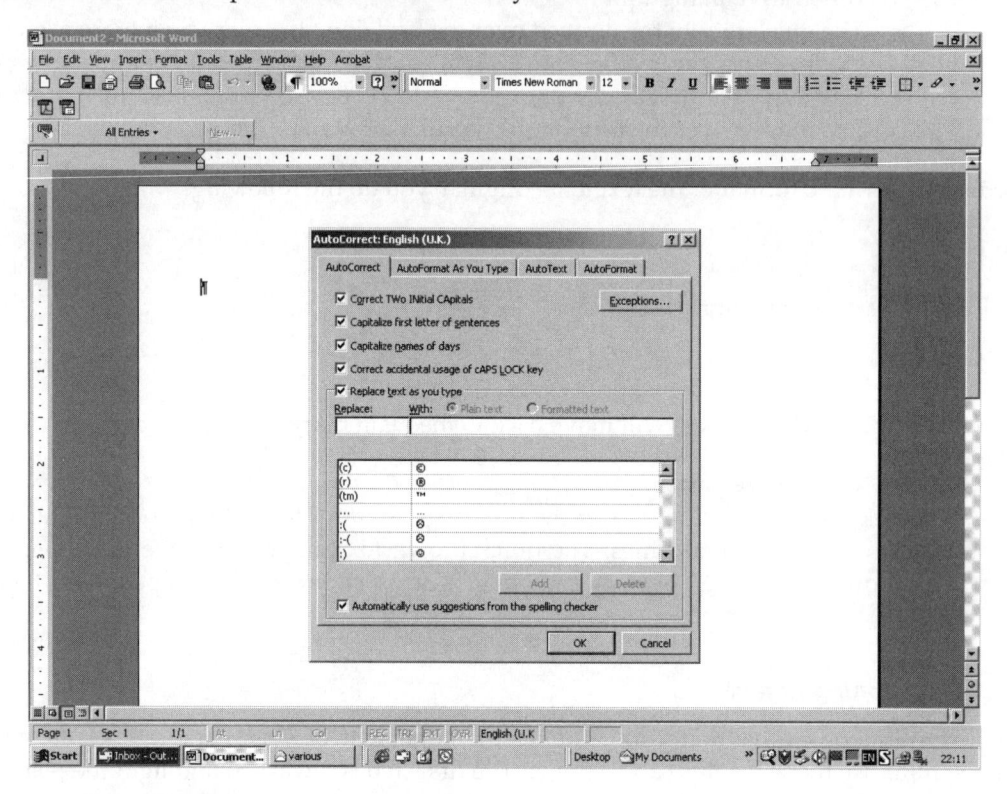

9 Spell check

The final Word feature we shall describe is one of the most useful. The spell check feature enables you to check the spelling of all the words in the document you have created. You use it as follows.

Step 1

Move the cursor to the start of the document.

Step 2

Press [F7]. A window will appear containing your document and highlighting the first word that the spell check feature considers to be mis-spelt. It gives you various suggestions on what the word should be, one of which it will have highlighted for you. It gives you various options such as 'change' or 'ignore' and you click on these as appropriate if you want to accept or reject the suggestion.

10 Quick quiz *(The answer is in the final chapter of this study text)*

1 Give three methods of adding up a column of numbers on an Excel spreadsheet.

2 Describe what these spreadsheet formulae will do:

    (i)   =(A6+B6)*17.5/100

    (ii)   =F7*F10/SUM(E1:E6)

3 How would you display cell contents of 1234.678 as 1,234.7?

11 Summary

You started by learning how to enter and exit the software package. Accessing any new software can be a daunting process for the novice, but with practise you will become very proficient in a short time. The main reason for accessing the package is to enter some data and process it somehow to produce the information required. This information should be produced in a format that is acceptable to the person who is to receive it.

You now understand how to improve the appearance of your spreadsheet by formatting individual cells. The examples given are only a few of the many ways in which the appearance of cells can be changed. You should experiment with others on a separate spreadsheet.

CHAPTER 8

Answers to chapter activities

Chapter 1

Activity 3

Materials		Labour		Expenses	
Choc chips	£150	Sewing machine operators	£800	Rent of building	£1,000
300m cloth	£2,500	Cake decorators time	£60	Electricity bill	£220
Cardboard cake boxes	£40				

Quick Quiz

1   The three main tasks of management are decision-making, planning and control.

2   A cost centre is a production or service location, function, activity or item of equipment for which costs can be determined.

3   A profit centre is a production or service location, function or activity for which costs and revenues can be determined.

4   Materials, labour and expenses.

Chapter 2

Activity 1

EDSP

Activity 2

(i)   110/124/201

(ii) 110/123/200

(iii) 111/120/202

(iv) 111/126/202

(v)   110/103/210

(vi) 110/125/201

UNIT 4 : SUPPLYING INFORMATION FOR MANAGEMENT CONTROL

Quick Quiz

1   A cost code is a system of symbols designed to be applied to a classified set of items, to give a brief accurate reference, which helps entry to the records, collation and analysis.

2   Any three of:

- To assist precise information
- To facilitate electronic data processing
- To facilitate a logical and systematic arrangement of costing records
- To simply comparison of totals of similar expenses
- To incorporate check codes

3   In practice costs are coded from the original documentation that is received when the costs are first recorded. This will include purchase invoices, cheque and cash payments and payments of wages and salaries by payroll.

Chapter 3

Activity 2

80 units × £3 = £240

Activity 3

Total weekly wage

	£
Monday (12 × £3)	36
Tuesday (14 × £3)	42
Wednesday (guarantee)	28
Thursday (14 × £3)	42
Friday (guarantee)	28
	176

The payment of a guaranteed amount is not a bonus for good work but simply an additional payment required if the amount of production is below a certain level.

Activity 4

The amount the employee will be paid will depend upon the exact wording of the agreement. Production of 102 units has taken the employee out of the lowest band (up to 99 units) and into the middle band (100 – 119 units). The question now is whether **all** his units are paid for at the middle rate (£1.50), or only the units produced in excess of 99. The two possibilities are as follows:

(a)   102 × £1.50 = £153.00

(b)   (99 × £1.25) + (3 × £1.50) = £128.25

Most organisations' agreements would apply method (b).

Output related pay is often known as piecework. Organisations paying employees in this manner normally operate a piecework with guarantee system or differential piecework systems.

Quick Quiz

1 A purchase requisition is completed before any goods are ordered to ensure that only goods that are required are purchased by the business.

2 When goods are received the stores department should check the details of the goods to the purchase order.

3 A purchase invoice should be checked to the purchase order to ensure that the goods were ordered and to the goods received note to check that they were received.

4 An overtime payment is the full payment for all overtime hours. The overtime premium is additional amount over and above the basic pay that is paid for the overtime hours.

5 Employer's NIC is normally classed as an expense.

6 The overtime premium is normally coded as an expense.

7 Factory workers working on the machines are direct labour. The factory supervisor is indirect labour.

8 Administrative expenses include rent and rates, telephone costs etc.

9 Apportionment

Chapter 4

Quick Quiz

1 Any three of:

- Processing orders from customer
- Negotiating the details of the order
- Notifying the production department of the order details
- Preparing the despatch note for the goods
- Preparing the sales invoice
- Organising the necessary advertising

2 Any three of:

- Advertising costs
- Transport expenses for delivering goods to customers
- Telephone costs
- Travelling expenses for the salesmen

Chapter 5

Activity 1

Labour cost – month 2

	Prior year £	Current year £	Increase/ (decrease) £
Production	336,000	510,000	174,000
Sales	248,000	350,000	102,000
Administration	100,000	130,000	30,000
Total	684,000	990,000	306,000

Activity 2

	Budgeted £	Actual £	Variance £
Labour	45,000	42,000	3,000 favourable
Material	60,000	62,000	2,000 adverse
Expenses	17,000	16,000	1,000 favourable

Quick Quiz

1 In a seasonal business it might not be useful to compare costs/income to the previous month rather than the same month in the previous year.

2 Debit   Work in progress control account

    Credit   Materials control account

3 Favourable variance

4 Adverse variance

Chapter 6

Quick Quiz

1 The key elements to be included in a memorandum are:

- Who it is to and from
- Date
- Reference
- Subject
- Main body
- Signature
- Names of any person the memo is to be copied to
- Details of any enclosures

Chapter 7

Activity 1

In the Excel worksheet that is used in this chapter it is IV65536.

Activity 2

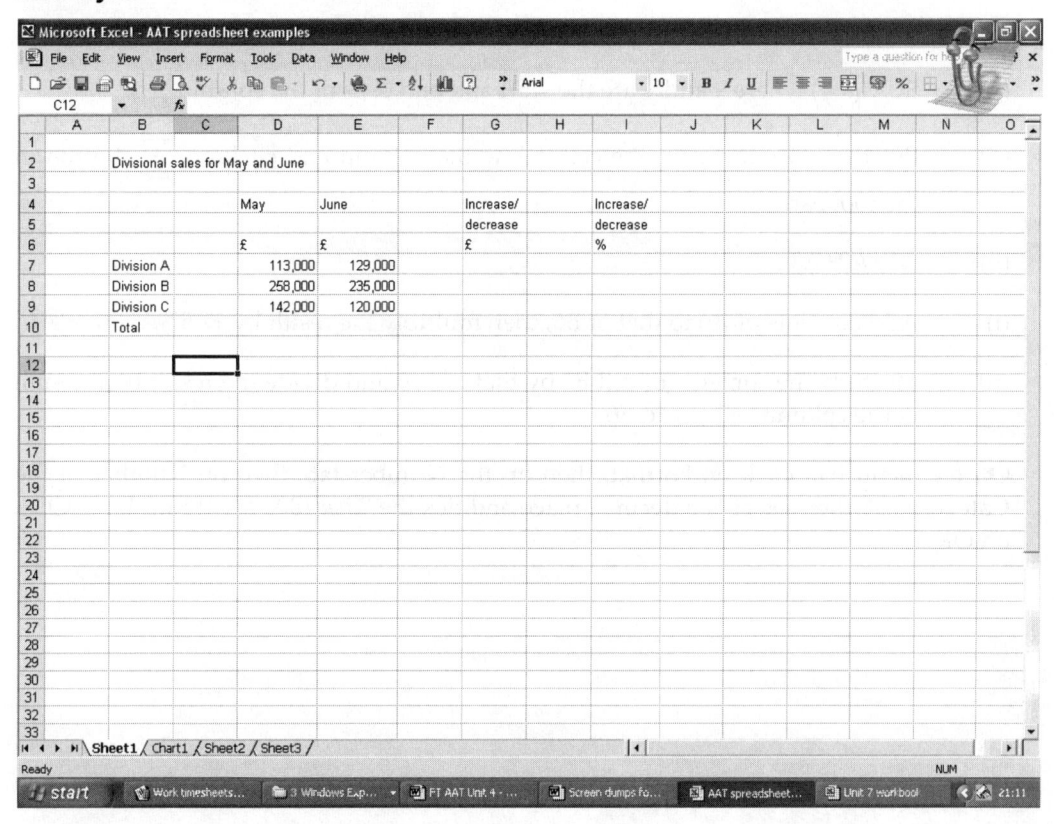

	A	B	C	D	E	F	G	H	I
1									
2		Divisional sales for May and June							
3									
4				May	June		Increase/		Increase/
5							decrease		decrease
6				£	£		£		%
7		Division A		113,000	129,000				
8		Division B		258,000	235,000				
9		Division C		142,000	120,000				
10		Total							

Activity 3

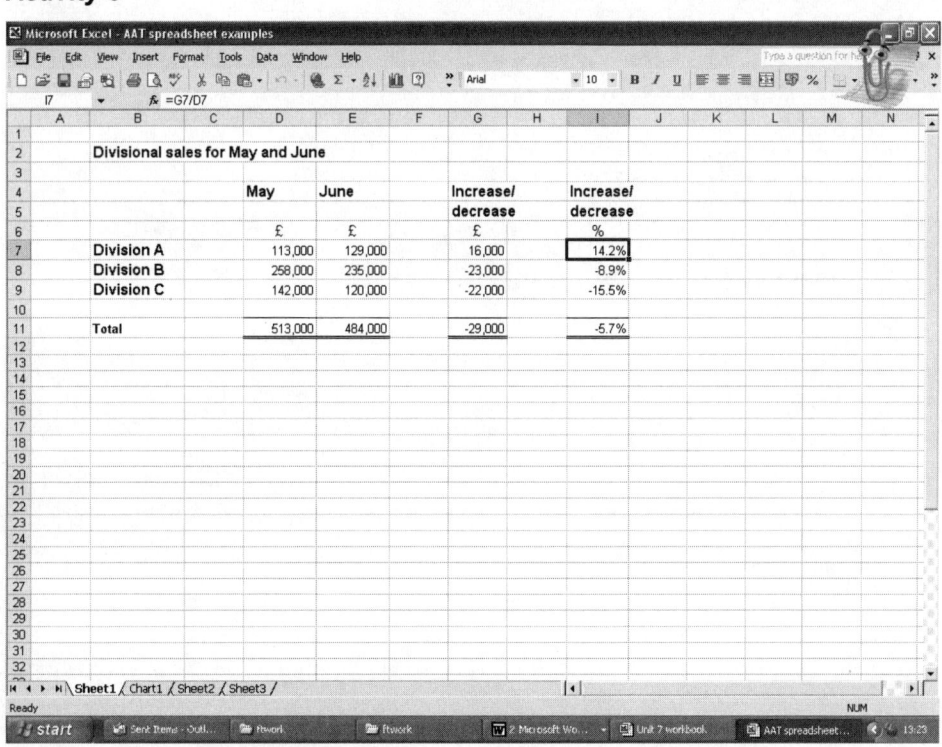

Cell I7 formula: =G7/D7

	A	B	C	D	E	F	G	H	I
1									
2		Divisional sales for May and June							
3									
4				May	June		Increase/		Increase/
5							decrease		decrease
6				£	£		£		%
7		Division A		113,000	129,000		16,000		14.2%
8		Division B		258,000	235,000		-23,000		-8.9%
9		Division C		142,000	120,000		-22,000		-15.5%
10									
11		Total		513,000	484,000		-29,000		-5.7%

The formulae used were:

In D11: =SUM(D7:D9)   In E11 =SUM(E7:E9)

In G7: = E7-D7   In G8: = E8-D8   In G9: E9-D9   In G11: = E11-D11

In 17: G7/E7   In 18: G8/E8   In 19: G9/E9   (all formatted to %age)

Quick Quiz

1   (i)   SUM(x:y) where x and y are the start and end cells of the column

    (ii)   Put the cell pointer on the cell below the column and click on $\sum$ button in the tool bar.

    (iii) A1+A2+A3 …..

2   (i)   Add contents of A6 to that of B6, then multiply the result by 17.5%.

    (ii)   Multiply the contents of cell F7 by that of F10 and divide the result by the sum of the column cells E1 to E6.

3   On the menu bar, click on Format, then on the Number tab, then on Number in the Category list, then select one decimal place and tick the 'Use 1000 separator' box. Click on OK.

WORKBOOK

KEY TECHNIQUES

QUESTION BANK

Key Techniques – Questions

Chapter 1
Introduction to management information

Activity 1
Explain the main differences between financial accounting and management accounting.

Activity 2
The main purpose of management accounting is to provide information to help management in three areas: decision-making, planning and control.'

Task

Briefly explain what is meant by decision-making, planning and control.

Activity 3
What might be the typical cost centres in each of the following types of organisation?

(a)   manufacturer of ready made meals

(b)   hospital

Chapter 2
Coding of costs and income

Activity 4
The expenses of an international organisation are coded with a seven digit code system as follows:

First and second digits	-	location
Third and fourth digits	-	function
Final three digits	-	type of expense

Extracts from within the costing system are as follows:

Location	Code
London	10
Dublin	11
Lagos	12
Nairobi	13
Kuala Lumpur	17
Hong Kong	18

UNIT 4 : SUPPLYING INFORMATION FOR MANAGEMENT CONTROL

Function	Code
Production	20
Marketing	21
Accounts	23
Administration	24

Type of expense	Code
Factory rent	201
Stationery	202
Telephone	203
Travel	204
Entertainment	205

Examples of the codes are as follows:

Factory rent in Nairobi:	1320201
Stationery purchased in London office:	1024202

Task 1

State the codes for the following items:

(a) Factory rent in the Dublin factory.

(b) Administration telephone costs incurred in Lagos.

(c) Salesman in Hong Kong entertaining an overseas visitor.

Task 2

State two advantages of using a coding system for the classification of costs and revenues.

Activity 5

The following is a simple example of how a code may be made up.

Type of material (Generic class)

1XX	Raw materials
2XX	Oils and lubricants
3XX	Indirect materials

Specific types of material within a generic class

X1X	Timber
X2X	Glue
X4X	Machine oil Grade 1
X5X	Machine oil Grade 2
X7X	Packaging material

X8X   Stationery

X9X   Petrol

Departmental utilisation (functional class)

XX1   Production - assembly

XX2   Production - packaging department

XX3   Sales department

XX4   Accounts department

Code 111   would represent wood used as a raw material in assembly production.

Code 252   would represent Grade 2 machine oil used to lubricate machines in the packaging department.

Task

What would codes 384, 293 and 172 represent?

Activity 6

Handels has recently appointed a stores controller who has decided to introduce a new stores control system. He has asked you to design a new material code for him.

Task 1

(a)   Briefly:

   (i)   describe the principles you feel should be observed when designing a materials classification code

   (ii)   state the advantages of such a coding in a system of stores control.

(b)   Assume that the design of your coding system has been completed. Included in the range of Handels' products is a series of flat sections of varying dimensions and in four different raw materials: Aluminium, Brass, Copper and Stainless Steel.

Material	Length	Thickness	Width	Code no.
Stainless steel	4'	$\frac{7}{8}"$	$3\frac{3}{4}"$	04081415
Brass	8'6"	$1\frac{3}{8}"$	2"	02172208

Task 2

Determine the code for the following

Aluminium $6'6" \times \frac{1}{4}" \times 3\frac{1}{2}"$

Copper $1' \times \frac{3}{8}" \times 3\frac{1}{4}"$

UNIT 4 : SUPPLYING INFORMATION FOR MANAGEMENT CONTROL

Task 3

Describe the type of bar as defined by these codes

01112903

03071721

Activity 7

A company manufactures shoes and slippers in half-sizes in the following ranges:

	Sizes
Mens	6 to 9½
Ladies	3 to 9
Boys	1 to 5½
Girls	1 to 5

The company uses a seven-digit code to identify its finished products, which, reading from left to right, is built up as follows:

Digit one indicates whether the products are mens, ladies, boys or girls. The numbers used are

1 - mens

2 - ladies

3 - boys

4 - girls

Digit two denotes type of footwear (shoes or slippers)

Digit three denotes colour (5 is green; 6 is burgundy)

Digit four denotes the material of the upper part of the product

Digit five denotes the material of the sole

Digits six and seven denote size.

Examples

(i) Code 1613275 represents a pair of mens slippers, brown suede, rubber sole, size 7½

(ii) Code 1324195 represents a pair of mens shoes, black leather, leather sole, size 9½

Task 1

Set suitable code numbers to the following, stating any assumptions you make:

(i) Boys shoes, brown leather uppers, rubber soles, size 4

(ii) Ladies slippers, green felt uppers, rubber soles, size 4½

(iii) Girls shoes, burgundy leather uppers, leather soles, size 3½.

Task 2

In connection with materials control, you are required to explain the following:

- The principles of coding
- four advantages of a coding system

Chapter 3
Materials, labour and expenses

Activity 8

Name the documents which you would consider important in the control and authorisation of material purchases.

Activity 9

An employee is paid a basic hourly rate of £4.40 per hour. The overtime payments are 1½ times the hourly rate.

Task

Calculate the amount paid for each hour of overtime.

Activity 10

An employee's basic rate of pay is £4.26 per hour and any overtime is paid at double rate. The basic hours per week are 38.

Task

An employee works 47 hours in a particular week. Calculate his pay for that week analysing the total into its basic and overtime premium components.

Activity 11

A division of a company has been allocated £10,000 to pay as an annual bonus to its 15 employees due to its good performance during the year.

Task

Calculate the bonus paid to each employee in the division if the bonus is to be allocated on a flat rate basis.

Activity 12

A division of a company has decided to pay an annual bonus to its 15 employees due to its good performance during the year.

Task

Calculate the bonus paid to an employee with an annual salary of £22,000 if the bonus is to be allocated on the basis of 2% of annual salary.

UNIT 4 : SUPPLYING INFORMATION FOR MANAGEMENT CONTROL

Activity 13

A Ltd makes engineering components. The company has been manufacturing 6,000 components per week, with six direct employees working a 40-hour week, at a basic wage of £4.00 per hour. Each worker operates independently.

A new remuneration scheme is being introduced. Each employee will receive payment on the following basis:

First 800 components per week	16 pence per unit
Next 200 components per week	17 pence per unit
All additional components per week	18 pence per unit

There will be a guaranteed minimum wage of £140.00 per week. It is expected that output will increase to 6,600 components per week with the new scheme.

Task

Describe the general features of time based and individual performance based remuneration systems, and outline the relative merits of each type of system.

(Use the above figures to illustrate your discussion, making whatever additional assumptions that you feel are necessary.)

Activity 14

Expenses are often termed as overheads and may be subdivided as; production, selling and distribution, administration and financial overhead.

Give three examples of each category.

Chapter 4
The selling function

Activity 15

Explain how the sales department of an organisation could be treated as a profit centre. Include explanation of the types of cost and income of the sales department.

Activity 16

Grendon Partners are an organisation that manufactures and sells mens clothing. The main categories of sales are casual wear (jeans and T shirts), business wear (suits, shirts and ties) and sportswear (shorts, tracksuits and sports tops). Sales are made from three separate retail outlets in Yandle, Smarden and Popham although the and daily sales summaries are processed centrally. An extract from the organisation's coding manual is given below:

Coding manual extract

Sales are given a six digit code. The first three digits relate to the outlet making the sale and the final three digits relate to the category of sale. The daily sales totalled for a week and used to update the sales coding listing.

KEY TECHNIQUES: QUESTIONS

Codes

Retail outlet

Yandle	100
Smarden	200
Popham	300

Category

Casual wear	400
Business wear	500
Sportswear	600

The daily sales listings for the last week of June for each of the outlets is given below:

Week commencing 25 June

Smarden outlet

	Mon	Tues	Wed	Thurs	Fri	Sat
	£	£	£	£	£	£
Casual wear	340	558	610	442	513	883
Business wear	120	140	155	254	189	330
Sportswear	540	389	125	443	515	772

Popham outlet

	Mon	Tues	Wed	Thurs	Fri	Sat
	£	£	£	£	£	£
Casual wear	132	234	438	753	746	442
Business wear	345	786	268	374	653	784
Sportswear	218	765	498	431	276	325

Yandle outlet

	Mon	Tues	Wed	Thurs	Fri	Sat
	£	£	£	£	£	£
Casual wear	545	789	230	785	645	650
Business wear	628	735	217	343	243	643
Sportswear	507	836	367	431	653	465

The sales coding listing for the month of June, as at Saturday 23 June, is given below. You are to update the sales coding listing for the sales made in the last week of June.

Sales coding listing

	To 23 June	Week commencing 25 June	Monthly total
	£	£	£
100400	9,320		
100500	5,456		
100600	10,429		
200400	8,345		
200500	3,104		
200600	8,246		
300400	7,245		
300500	10,440		
300600	7,324		

FTC FOULKS LYNCH

UNIT 4 : SUPPLYING INFORMATION FOR MANAGEMENT CONTROL

Chapter 5
Comparison of information

Activity 17

Define the terms:

- Budget

- Variance.

Activity 18

Hockeyskill Ltd manufacture hockey sticks and divides its sales function into four main areas:

(1) Scotland and the North

(2) Midlands

(3) South East

(4) South West.

Its cumulative sales for five months ended 20X3 and actual sales for June were:

		Jan-May £	June £
Area	1	31,000	7,100
	2	33,500	8,200
	3	49,000	9,750
	4	41,000	8,210
		£154,500	£33,260

The budget for the six months was:

		£
Area	1	37,500
		40,500
		57,500
		46,500
		£182,000

Task

Prepare a statement for management to show the budget and actual sales for each sales area for the six months ended 30 June showing clearly the variance for each area and in total.

Activity 19

Northcliffe Feeds produce animal feed. It has three main products: A1 Plus, B Plus and Feed Plus. Its planned production and sales for the quarter ended 30 June 20X3 (budgeted) was:

	Sales tonnes	Selling price per tonne £
A1 Plus	12,000	100
B Plus	11,000	120
Feed Plus	9,500	125

Actual sales for the quarter ended 30 June 20X3:

	Sales tonnes	Sales value
A1 Plus	12,600	£1,272,600
B Plus	11,000	£1,331,000
Feed Plus	9,000	£1,116,000

Tasks

- Present a statement to management to show, for each product and in total, the budgeted sales value and the actual sales value and the variance for each.

- Calculate for each product the average actual selling price per tonne.

- Calculate the percentage increase or decrease on the budgeted selling price per tonne per product for the period.

- Present a statement showing for each product and in total the budget and actual tonnage for the period.

Activity 20

The costs of production of a business for the months of April 20X1 and April 20X0 are given below:

	April 20X1 £	April 20X0 £
Materials	253,400	244,300
Labour	318,200	302,600
Expenses	68,700	72,400

Draw up a table showing the difference between the costs of the current month and of the corresponding month in £s, and as a percentage of the April 20X0 costs.

Activity 21

Given below are the budgeted and actual costs for the two production cost centres of a business for May 20X1.

	Budget £	Actual £
Cost centre 1		
Materials	48,700	46,230
Labour	37,600	39,940
Expenses	5,200	3,700
Cost centre 2		
Materials	56,200	62,580
Labour	22,500	20,400
Expenses	4,800	5,600

You are required to draw up a table showing the amount of the variances for the month. You are also to indicate which variances should be reported to management if it is the business's policy to report only variances that are more than 15% of the budgeted figure.

Chapter 6
Reporting

Activity 22

For each of the following tasks, state what would be the most appropriate reporting medium to use – a note, a letter, a memorandum or a report.

(a) Information to be provided to the management accountant regarding absenteeism in the factory for the last three years.

(b) Information for a colleague in the accounting department regarding the code for sales of a particular product.

(c) A request for annual holiday to be sent to the head of your department.

(d) A reply to a supplier regarding problems with delivery dates.

(e) Details of the stock levels of a raw material requested by the cost accountant.

Chapter 7
Spreadsheets

Activity 23

The manager of a small flower shop, Petalart, is preparing a cash flow forecast for the coming three months, and has gathered the following information:

Sales in September were £3,600, and are expected to be £3,750 in each of October and November and £4,800 in December. Most customers pay when they buy, but it is estimated that 20% of the sales are made to corporate customers, who pay in the month following that of sale.

The costs of flower and other purchases account for 50% of sales values, and are paid on a cash on delivery basis. The costs of the shop, staff etc come to £1,200 per month., also paid in the month they are incurred.

The bank balance at 30 September is expected to be £450.

The cash flow forecast proforma is as follows:

	October	November	December	Total
	£	£	£	£
Sales	3,750	3,750	4,800	
Receipts – from current month's sales				
– from previous month's sales				
Total receipts				
Purchase costs				
Fixed costs				
Total payments				
Net cashflow				
Bank balance b/f				
Bank balance c/f				

Set up a spreadsheet to compute the end of month cash balances.

PRACTICE SIMULATIONS

Practice Simulation 1 – Questions

The situation

Your name is Parfraz Mehdi, and you are an Accounts Assistant working for Avontree Limited, Unit 5, Burberry Business Park, Newfields NF8 2PR. Avontree is a publisher of textbooks used in primary, secondary and higher education. You report to the Accounts Supervisor, Emily Padden.

Coding of original documents

Avontree's accounts are maintained on a simple computerised system. One of your responsibilities is to code original documents for entry onto this system. For example, you code both sales and purchase invoices and enter relevant details onto data input sheets, which are then used for entering data into the computer system. In some cases you delegate the original coding to a colleague.

Payroll is maintained by Emily Padden on a computerised system separate from the accounts system. Each month she provides you with a payroll printout. Your task is to enter the appropriate codes for posting to the accounts system.

When doing your coding, you will need to refer to the company's policy manual; see page 10 of this booklet for relevant extracts. The purpose of the coding is to allocate costs and revenues to the appropriate cost and revenue centres, and also to distinguish between different types of costs and revenues.

VAT

Coding of VAT is performed automatically by the computerised accounts system, and therefore it is the amount before VAT on a purchase invoice that needs to be coded. There is no VAT on Avontree's sales invoices because textbooks are zero-rated.

The date

In this simulation you will be dealing with transactions arising in May and June 20X3.

Today's date is 9 June 20X3.

UNIT 4 : SUPPLYING INFORMATION FOR MANAGEMENT CONTROL

The tasks to be completed

Task 1 On the next few pages you will find eight sales invoices items (see item 2).

- Enter relevant details of the sales invoices, including appropriate codes, on the data input sheet (item 5 in the answer booklet). You will need to refer to the extract from the company's policy manual on the following pages (see item 1).

Task 2 On the following pages you will find purchase invoices (item 3) received from Avontree's suppliers, and related purchase orders raised by Avontree. The purchase invoices have already been coded by one of your colleagues.

- Check the purchase invoices to ensure that they match the purchase orders, and also check that your colleague has entered the correct codes on the invoices. You will need to refer to the extract from the company's policy manual (item 1).

- Your checks should reveal discrepancies. Draft an email to Emily Padden describing these discrepancies. Use the blank email window (Item 6 in theanswer booklet).

Task 3 The payroll printout for May 20X3 is enclosed (item 4)

- Enter the appropriate amounts and codes on the input sheet (item 7), ready for inputting the payroll details to the accounts system.

Task 4 Refer to the report (item 8). This has been extracted from the accounts system and shows the year-to-date (YTD) totals for certain revenue and expenditure accounts up to the end of May 20X3, along with comparative figures for the previous year.

- In the column headed 'Variance (£)', enter the monetary amount of the variance enter the monetary amount of the variance between this year and last, using the symbol '+' to indicate an increase over last year and the symbol '–' to indicate a decrease compared with last year.

- In the column headed 'Variance (%)' enter each variance as a percentage of last year's total, again using the symbols '+' and '–' and expressing the percentages to one decimal place.

(To guide you, the first line of the schedule has already been completed.)

Task 5 Draft a brief report using the blank report in the answer booklet (Item 9) to Emily Padden, to which you will attach the schedule you prepared in Task 4. Draw her attention to any instances where the calculated variance exceeds 5%. Date your report 9 June 20X3.

Item 1 Policy Manual (extracts)

Coding of sales revenue

Each item of sales revenue must be coded with two pieces of information:

- the revenue centre (see below);
- the type of revenue (see below).

The type of revenue is indicated by the product code. Textbooks for primary education have codes beginning with P. Textbooks for secondary education have codes beginning with S. Textbooks for higher education have codes beginning with H.

Only the net goods value is coded (i.e. the value of goods after deduction of trade discount).

Revenue centres

UK sales	100
Overseas sales	200

Types of revenue

Textbook sales: primary education	300
Textbook sales: secondary education	400
Textbook sales: higher education	500

Coding of expenditure

Each item of expenditure must be coded with two pieces of information:

- the cost centre (see below);
- the type of expenditure (see below).

Cost centres

Typesetting costs	610
Editing costs	620
Printing and binding costs	630
Distribution and despatch costs	640
Marketing costs	650
Establishment costs	660

Types of cost

Materials	710
Expenses	720
Salaries	730

The costs of services performed by external individuals or organisations are classified as 'expenses'. The costs of paying internal staff are classified as 'salaries'. All salaries are classified to the 'establishment costs' cost centre.

Item 2 Sales Invoices

SALES INVOICE
Avontree Limited
Unit 5, Burberry Business Park, Newfields NF8 2PR

Invoice to:
Megabooks Limited
33 High Street
Maidenhead SL6 1PQ
UK

VAT Registration: 225 6712 89
Date/tax point: 5 June 20X3
Invoice number: 52711

Titles supplied	Item code	Quantity	List price (£)	Total (£)
GCSE Mathematics	S2251	10	12.50	125.00
Intermediate Mathematics	S1201	12	5.50	66.00

Total at list price	191.00
Less trade discount @ 35%	66.85
Net goods value	124.15
VAT @ 0%	0.00
Total due	**124.15**

Terms: net 30 days

SALES INVOICE
Avontree Limited
Unit 5, Burberry Business Park, Newfields NF8 2PR

Invoice to:
Books Plus
102 Lampard Avenue
Bristol BS3 5EW
UK

VAT Registration: 225 6712 89
Date/tax point: 5 June 20X3
Invoice number: 52712

Titles supplied	Item code	Quantity	List price (£)	Total (£)
Applications of Electronics	H3141	4	27.00	108.00
Thermodynamics	H2278	2	32.50	65.00

Total at list price	173.00
Less trade discount @ 40%	69.20
Net goods value	103.80
VAT @ 0%	0.00
Total due	**103.80**

Terms: net 30 days

SALES INVOICE
Avontree Limited
Unit 5, Burberry Business Park, Newfields NF8 2PR

Invoice to:
Empstone Books Ltd
14 Cygnet Street
Holyport SO13 7KK
UK

VAT Registration: 225 6712 89
Date/tax point: 5 June 20X3
Invoice number: 52713

Titles supplied	Item code	Quantity	List price (£)	Total (£)
The Metres of English Poetry	S1190	3	16.00	48.00
Tudor History for Teenagers	S3124	6	14.00	84.00
The Stuarts: a Brief Survey	S5155	6	14.00	84.00

Total at list price	216.00
Less trade discount @ 32.5%	70.20
Net goods value	145.80
VAT @ 0%	0.00
Total due	**145.80**

Terms: net 30 days

SALES INVOICE
Avontree Limited
Unit 5, Burberry Business Park, Newfields NF8 2PR

Invoice to:
Win Hong Books
17 Swire Street
Central
HONG KONG

VAT Registration: 225 6712 89
Date/tax point: 5 June 20X3
Invoice number: 52714

Titles supplied	Item code	Quantity	List price (£)	Total (£)
Daily Life in Ancient Egypt	P9124	20	6.20	124.00
Daily Life in Ancient Rome	P9130	20	6.20	124.00

Total at list price	248.00
Less trade discount @ 35%	86.80
Net goods value	161.20
VAT @ 0%	0.00
Total due	**161.20**

Terms: net 30 days

SALES INVOICE
Avontree Limited
Unit 5, Burberry Business Park, Newfields NF8 2PR

Invoice to:
Tradesales Limited
65 Limetree Avenue
Birkenhead WA12 5TR
UK

VAT Registration: 225 6712 89
Date/tax point: 5 June 20X3
Invoice number: 52715

Titles supplied	Item code	Quantity	List price (£)	Total (£)
GCSE Mathematics	S2251	4	12.50	50.00
A level Mathematics	S1452	10	15.00	150.00

Total at list price	200.00
Less trade discount @ 40%	80.00
Net goods value	120.00
VAT @ 0%	0.00
Total due	**120.00**

Terms: net 30 days

SALES INVOICE
Avontree Limited
Unit 5, Burberry Business Park, Newfields NF8 2PR

Invoice to:
Palmer and Company
18 Ambleden Avenue
Rystone
UK

VAT Registration: 225 6712 89
Date/tax point: 5 June 20X3
Invoice number: 52716

Titles supplied	Item code	Quantity	List price (£)	Total (£)
GCSE French	S4123	20	12.80	256.00
GCSE Spanish	S4145	16	12.80	204.80

Total at list price	460.80
Less trade discount @ 35%	161.28
Net goods value	299.52
VAT @ 0%	0.00
Total due	**299.52**

Terms: net 30 days

PRACTICE SIMULATION 1: **ANSWER BOOKLET**

SALES INVOICE
Avontree Limited
Unit 5, Burberry Business Park, Newfields NF8 2PR

Invoice to:
Business Books
18 High Street
Hensham CV28 5AP
UK

VAT Registration: 225 6712 89
Date/tax point: 5 June 20X3
Invoice number: 52717

Titles supplied	Item code	Quantity	List price (£)	Total (£)
Management Principles and Practice	H3121	8	26.50	212.00
Total at list price
Less trade discount @ 30%				212.00
63.60
Net goods value
VAT @ 0%				148.40
0.00
Total due				**148.40**

Terms: net 30 days

SALES INVOICE
Avontree Limited
Unit 5, Burberry Business Park, Newfields NF8 2PR

Invoice to:
Megabooks Limited
33 High Street
Maidenhead SL6 1PQ
UK

VAT Registration: 225 6712 89
Date/tax point: 5 June 20X3
Invoice number: 52718

Titles supplied	Item code	Quantity	List price (£)	Total (£)
En Avant: French for Beginners	S2234	22	16.00	352.00
Total at list price
Less trade discount @ 35%				352.00
123.20
Net goods value
VAT @ 0%				228.80
0.00
Total due				**228.80**

Terms: net 30 days

FTC FOULKS LYNCH

UNIT 4 : SUPPLYING INFORMATION FOR MANAGEMENT CONTROL

Item 3 Purchase Invoices

SALES INVOICE
The Boxshop
25 Lyme Street, Taunton, TA2 4RP

Invoice to:
Avontree Limited

Unit 5
Burberry Business Park
Newfields NF8 2PR

VAT Registration:	254 1781 26
Date/tax point:	5 June 20X3
Invoice number:	288712
Your order:	2305

Description of goods/services	Total (£)
2,000 postal despatch boxes, PDB 126	765.00

Amount (£)	Cost centre/revenue centre	Expenditure/revenue type
765.00	640	710

Goods total	765.00
VAT @ 17.5%	133.87
Total due	**898.87**

Terms: net 30 days

SALES INVOICE
Editype Limited
28 Wakeland Road, Newfields NF4 7LK

Invoice to:
Avontree Limited

Unit 5
Burberry Business Park
Newfields NF8 2PR

VAT Registration:	267 9912 46
Date/tax point:	5 June 20X3
Invoice number:	2511

Description of goods/services	Total (£)
Editorial work to your specification on *Corporate Strategy*	400.00

Amount (£)	Cost centre/revenue centre	Expenditure/revenue type
400.00	620	720

Total at list price	400.00
VAT @ 17.5%	70.00
Total due	**470.00**

Terms: net 30 days

SALES INVOICE
Education Magazine
17 Britton Street, London EC1M 5TP

Invoice to:
Avontree Limited

Unit 5
Burberry Business Park
Newfields NF8 2PR

VAT Registration: 315 8123 49
Date/tax point: 5 June 20X3
Invoice number: 22111098
Your order: 2259

Description of goods/services	Total (£)
Sales advertisement in June 2003 issue	870.00

Amount (£)	Cost centre/revenue centre	Expenditure/revenue type
870.00	650	720

Total at list price	870.00
VAT @ 17.5%	152.25
Total due	**1,022.25**

Terms: net 30 days

SALES INVOICE
Litho Printing Limited
Rosina Street, London E8 7RT

Invoice to:
Avontree Limited

Unit 5
Burberry Business Park
Newfields NF8 2PR

VAT Registration: 412 5512 38
Date/tax point: 5 June 20X3
Invoice number: 217765
Your order: 2271

Description of goods/services	Total (£)
Printing and binding 5,000 copies of *The War of the Roses*	16,410.00

Amount (£)	Cost centre/revenue centre	Expenditure/revenue type
16,410.00	630	710

Total at list price	16,410.00
VAT: zero-rated	0.00
Total due	**16,410.00**

Terms: net 30 days

UNIT 4 : SUPPLYING INFORMATION FOR MANAGEMENT CONTROL

SALES INVOICE
Typetext Limited
21 Ashton Lane, Newfields NF2 7UT

Invoice to:
Avontree Limited

Unit 5
Burberry Business Park
Newfields NF8 2PR

VAT Registration: 251 7171 34
Date/tax point: 5 June 20X3
Invoice number: 276
Your order: 2286

Description of goods/services	Total (£)
Typesetting of *GCSE Geography* to agreed specification	1,200.00
Total at list price	1,200.00
VAT @ 17.5%	210.00
Total due	**1,410.00**

Amount (£)	Cost centre/ revenue centre	Expenditure/ revenue type
1,200.00	610	720

Terms: net 30 days

SALES INVOICE
Decofix limited
Panton Close, Newfields NF8 2PR

Invoice to:
Avontree Limited

Unit 5
Burberry Business Park
Newfields NF8 2PR

VAT Registration: 381 5512 60
Date/tax point: 5 June 20X3
Invoice number: 198
Your order: 2268

Description of goods/services	Total (£)
Repainting of accounts office to agreed specification	312.00
Total at list price	312.00
VAT @ 17.5%	54.60
Total due	**366.60**

Amount (£)	Cost centre/ revenue centre	Expenditure/ revenue type
312.00	660	710

Terms: net 30 days

PRACTICE SIMULATION 1: ANSWER BOOKLET

PURCHASE ORDER
Avontree Limited
Unit 5, Burberry Business Park,
Newfields NF8 2PR

To: Litho Printing Limited Rosina Street London E8 7RT	Date: 13 May 20X3 Order no: 2271

Please supply the items/services below on the agreed terms.

Quantity	Description	Item code
500	Bound copies of *The War of the Roses*	N/A

On behalf of Avontree Limited
Emily Padden

PURCHASE ORDER
Avontree Limited
Unit 5, Burberry Business Park,
Newfields NF8 2PR

To: The Boxshop 25 Lyme Street Taunton TA2 4RP	Date: 20 May 20X3 Order no: 2305

Please supply the items/services below on the agreed terms.

Quantity	Description	Item code
2,000	Postal despatch boxes	PDB126

On behalf of Avontree Limited
Emily Padden

PURCHASE ORDER
Avontree Limited
Unit 5, Burberry Business Park,
Newfields NF8 2PR

To: Decofix Limited Panton Close Newfields NF6 3QT	Date: 12 May 20X3 Order no: 2268

Please supply the items/services below on the agreed terms.

Quantity	Description	Item code
1	Repainting of accounts office to agreed specification	N/A

On behalf of Avontree Limited
Emily Padden

PURCHASE ORDER
Avontree Limited
Unit 5, Burberry Business Park,
Newfields NF8 2PR

To: Typestext Limited 21 Ashton Lane Newfields NF2 7UT	Date: 16 May 20X3 Order no: 2286

Please supply the items/services below on the agreed terms.

Quantity	Description	Item code
1	Typesetting of *GCSE Geography* to agreed specification	N/A

On behalf of Avontree Limited
Emily Padden

UNIT 4 : SUPPLYING INFORMATION FOR MANAGEMENT CONTROL

```
          PURCHASE ORDER
            Avontree Limited
       Unit 5, Burberry Business Park,
            Newfields NF8 2PR
```

To:		
Education Magazine	Date:	9 May 20X3
17 Britton Street	Order no:	2259
London EC1M 5TP		

Please supply the items/services below on the agreed terms.

Quantity	Description	Item code
1	Sales advertisement in June 2003 issue	N/A

On behalf of Avontree Limited
Emily Padden

Item 4 Salaries Summary

Month: May 20X3

Employee name	Gross pay (£)	PAYE tax (£)	Employee NIC (£)	Net pay (£)	Employer NIC (£)
James Bailey	850.00	91.00	46.60	712.40	54.99
Laura Drinkwater	3,000.00	572.00	215.00	2,213.00	308.57
Allan Holmes	1,250.00	189.00	86.60	974.40	102.19
Caroline Johnson	1,000.00	139.00	61.40	799.60	72.45
Parfraz Mehdi	1,400.00	225.00	101.40	1,073.60	119.65
Emily Padden	2,300.00	418.00	191.40	1,690.60	225.85
Roland White	1,100.00	157.00	71.40	871.60	84.25
	10,900.00	1,791.00	773.80	8,335.20	967.95

Practice Simulation 1 – Answer booklet

Item 5 (for Task 1)

DATA INPUT SHEET

Sales invoices   Date: _____

Invoice number	Customer	Coding		
		Amount £	Revenue centre	Type of revenue

Item 6 (for Task 2)

EMAIL
From:
To:
CC:
Subject:
Date:
Message

FTC FOULKS LYNCH

Item 7 (for Task 3)

DATA INPUT SHEET

Payroll   Date: _____

| Detail | Coding |||
	Amount £	Cost centre	Type of expenditure

Item 8 (for Task 4)

Avontree Limited

Profit and loss account

Date: 31 May 20X3

Account code	Account name	YTD This year	YTD Last year	Variance £	Variance %
100–300	UK sales: primary	75,600	74,100	+1,500	+2.0
100–400	UK sales: secondary	100,900	108,700		
100–500	UK sales: higher	98,700	95,000		
610–720	Typesetting: expenses	15,300	16,000		
620–720	Editing: expenses	16,400	15,700		
630–710	Printing & binding: materials	40,100	36,500		
640–710	Distribution: materials	4,600	6,100		
650–720	Marketing: expenses	16,400	15,900		
660–720	Establishment: expenses	5,600	5,200		
660–730	Establishment: salaries	34,200	33,000		

Item 9 (for Task 5)

REPORT

To:
From:
Subject:
Date:

Practice Simulation 2 – Questions

The situation

Your name is Candy Date and you work as an accounts assistant in the administration department of "Cards-R-Us", a producer of greeting cards.

You report to the management accountant, Thelma Jones. Your work is on a monthly cycle, with other projects being given to you by Thelma Jones at various times. Your main tasks are coding income and expenditure from all source documents and preparing performance reports. A junior assistant, Liam Green, sometimes helps you during busy periods.

Today's date is 12 September 20X3.

"Cards –R-Us" makes three types of cards:

- birthday cards
- christmas cards
- special occasion cards

Sales are recorded in the following profit centres:

- United kingdom
- Europe
- U.S.A.
- Rest of the World

Production is organised into the following cost centres:

- printing
- cutting
- wrapping
- packing

Production is serviced by the following cost centres:

- administration
- stores
- marketing and distribution
- maintenance

The Coding System

The coding system for the company is based on a three-digit system.

The first digit denotes the type of income or expenditure:

1   profit centre income

2   cost centre expenditure

3   asset expenditure
4   liabilities
5   capital

Profit Centres

The profit centres are coded as follows:

110   United Kingdom

120   Europe

130   U.S.A.

140   Rest of the World

The third digit denotes the type of sale:

001   birthday card

002   Christmas card

003   special occasion cards

This means that the sale of birthday cards in Europe would be coded 121.

Cost Centres

The cost centres are coded as follows:

210	printing	250	administration
220	cutting	260	stores
230	wrapping	270	marketing and distribution
240	packing	280	maintenance

The third digit donates the type of expenditure:

001   material
002   labour

003   expenses

This means that the rent expenditure of the wrapping department would be 233.

Performance Reports

The performance reports that you prepare on a monthly basis are for the:

- management accountant

- sales director

- production director

- cost centre managers

- profit centre managers

The tasks to be completed

Task 1 Refer to the sales and purchases invoices (item 1).

Code these invoices by completing the coding extract for income and expenditure (item 5 in the answer booklet). For each relevant code you should post the amendment and update the balance. Ignore the VAT element (this is coded automatically upon receipt of the invoice).

Task 2 You receive the memo (item 2) from a cost centre manager about a wage payment that has been missed in the packing department for the month of August 20X3.

Read the memo and then do the following:

- complete the wage payment schedule (item 6) to the nearest penny.
- amend the coding extract (item 5) and update the relevant codes to the nearest £.

Note: Basic pay coded to labour and other employee costs are expenses.

Task 3 Liam Green has left on your desk the three invoices shown (item 4) together with the note shown (item 3).

Review the note and the three invoices and then write a memo to Liam Green using the blank memo in the answer booklet (item 7). The memo should advise him:

- of any mistakes in checking and coding that have been made
- of the appropriate persons that he needs to contact to get the information to carry out the correct coding.

Date the memo 12 September 20X3.

Task 4 In item 8 you will find a list of ledger balances for the year to date to 31 July 20X3.

Update this to 31 August 20X3 by posting the amended coding extract that you have completed in item 5.

Task 5 Using your answer from Task 4, complete the performance report for total costs of the production cost centres in item 9.

Task 6 Thelma has asked that you report to her any production cost variance of more than 10% from budget, either for the year to date or for the month of August 20X3.

Using your answer to Task 5, complete the discrepancy (variance) report (item 10), and then use the comment section to identify the significant variances that Thelma has asked for.

Task 7 Using your answer to Task 4, complete the sales performance report for total sales (item 11).

Task 8 Joan Standard, the Sales Director, is new in the post and the sales performance report that you completed in Task 7 and sent to her is the first that she has received from you. Liam has taken a message from her asking you to phone her back to tell her:

- what you see as the key purpose of the report
- what uses it can be put to
- what other information can be provided from the data that you have available.

List the key points (see item 12) that you see as the basis of the telephone conversation that you will have with her.

UNIT 4 : SUPPLYING INFORMATION FOR MANAGEMENT CONTROL

Item 1 Sales and Purchase Invoices

"CARDS R US"		
SAFFRON DRIVE	VAT:	241162208
WEST WALFORD	TEL NO:	07 421 316
SALOPS	FAX NO:	07 421 317
SA49LK	TAX POINT:	30 AUG 20X3

SALES INVOICE

INVOICE NO: 28417

TO
CARD WAREHOUSE LTD
18 ROLLOVER DRIVE
TOSCAN
WORKBURG U.S.A.

DETAILS	NO.	NET £	TOTAL £
Type A Birthday Cards	2,000	0.80	1,600.00
Type C Wedding Cards	3,000	1.00	3,000.00
TOTAL BEFORE VAT			4,600.00
VAT			0.00
TOTAL INCLUDING VAT			4,600.00

"CARDS R US"		
SAFFRON DRIVE	VAT:	241162208
WEST WALFORD	TEL NO:	07 421 316
SALOPS	FAX NO:	07 421 317
SA49LK	TAX POINT:	30 AUG 20X3

SALES INVOICE

INVOICE NO: 29124

TO
SURESHOP LTD
17 RUE DU PARIS
PARIS
FRANCE

DETAILS	NO.	NET £	TOTAL £
Type C Christmas Cards	2,000	0.85	1,700.00
Type D Engagement Cards	4,000	0.95	3,800.00
TOTAL BEFORE VAT			5,500.00
VAT			0.00
TOTAL INCLUDING VAT			5,500.00

TRANWAY PRINTING			
35 Holding Way		Invoice No:	6195
Whippleton		VAT No:	246 368 241
Leics		Tax Point:	30/08/20X3
LE9 2NR		Tel No:	01567 78645
		Fax No:	01567 78646

INVOICE TO

Cards R Us
Saffron Drive
West Walford
Salops
SA4 9LK

	£
100 rolls of cards at £8.90 per roll to be delivered to your Cutting Department	890.00
300 fabric prints at £2.50 per print, to be delivered to your Print Department	750.00
VAT	287.00
Total including VAT	1,927.00

D.A.Associates			
22 Catlin Road		Invoice No:	2167
York Avenue		VAT No:	310 861 143
Maidstone		Tax Point:	26/08/20X3
Kent MA9 4CL		Tel No:	01234 862178
		Fax No:	01234 862179

INVOICE TO

Cards R Us
Saffron Drive
West Walford
Salops
SA4 9LK

	£
Maintenance Contract for the machines in your wrapping Dept. For the year ending 31 July 20X4	1,500.00
VAT	262.50
Total including VAT	1,762.50

UNIT 4 : SUPPLYING INFORMATION FOR MANAGEMENT CONTROL

Item 2 Memo

MEMO

To: Candy Date, Accounts Assistant

From: John Steel, Packing Department Manager

Date: 11 September 20X3

Subject: Missed wage payment

We missed a wage payment for John White, an operative on one of our packing machines, for the last week of August 20X3. He worked 35 hours at a rate of £8 per hour and then did 8 hours of overtime at time and a half to clear a general backlog.

Please calculate and code the basic wage payment and employee costs and then pass the details on to the payroll department for the personal deductions. He is a full time employee so the employer's pension contribution of 6% of basic wage payment applies, as does the employer's national insurance contribution of 12% above £84 per week.

Thanks

Item 3 Note

NOTEPAD

Candy

I have just checked and coded the attached invoices for September 20X3 but I am not sure whether the action I have taken is correct. Please help!

Liam

Item 4 Invoices

Ince and Sons Brokers

2 Lambert Avenue
Bristol
BR9 6EL

Invoice No: 2167

Tel No: 01717 733451

Invoice to:
Cards R Us
Saffron Drive
West Walford
Salops
SA4 9LK

(213)

Provision of insurance for your factory for the year ending 30 September 20X4 — £6,000.00

Aftercare Limited

13 Carson Road
London
20X3
SN4 0EL

Invoice No: 1468
VAT No: 789 453 292
Tax Point: 11 September

Tel No: 020 7941 367

Invoice to:
Cards Delight
27 Wapping Lane
Portsmouth
Hants
PO1 9FM

(253)

Provision of temporary staff for your Admin Department

8 days at £150 per day   £1,200

Cellplate Ltd

Unit 6,
Dockway Drive,
20X3
Liverpool LA4 5XF

Invoice No: 4736
VAT No: 241 074 375
Tax Point: 4 September

Tel No: 0151 441 857

Invoice to:
Cards R Us
Saffron Drive   213
West Walford
Salops
SA4 9LK

(231)

48 boxes of wrapping material at £25 per box   £12,000

Practice Simulation 2 – Answer booklet

Item 5 (for Tasks 1&2)

CODING EXTRACT – INCOME AND EXPENDITURE – AUGUST 20X3
(ROUNDED TO NEAREST £)

Code	Balance (£)	Amendment (£)	Updated Balance (£)
111	38,916		
112	27,413		
113	33,476		
121	42,457		
122	29,376		
123	24,294		
131	38,462		
132	34,761		
133	37,314		
141	41,694		
142	52,316		
143	45,761		
211	47,412		
212	11,467		
213	20,439		
221	43,764		
222	11,461		
223	15,064		
231	8,216		
232	4,916		
233	9,074		
241	3,642		
242	4,164		
243	7,695		
253	6,613		
263	7,008		
273	6,744		
283	4,539		

UNIT 4 : SUPPLYING INFORMATION FOR MANAGEMENT CONTROL

Item 6 (for Task 2)

	PAYROLL CALCULATION		
	AUGUST 20X3		
NAME			
DEPARTMENT			
BASIC RATE			
HOURS WORKED			
HOURS FOR OVERTIME PREMIUM			
	Calculation	Amount (£)	Code
BASIC RATE			
OVERTIME PREMIUM			
EMPLOYERS PENSION CONT.			
EMPLOYERS N.I.C.			
TOTALS FOR POSTING	Code	Amount (£)	

Item 7 (for Task 3)

MEMO

To:
From:
Date:
Subject:

Item 8 (for Task 4)

INCOME AND EXPENDITURE BALANCES – Year Ending 31/12/20X3

Ledger Account	Bal. At 31/7/20X3	Amt. Coded Aug 20X3	Bal. At 31/8/20X3
Sales	£	£	£
Birthday Cards			
- UK	245,365		
-Europe	198,467		
-U.S.A.	231,989		
-R. of W.	297,946		
Christmas Cards			
- UK	246,578		
-Europe	316,478		
-U.S.A.	297,697		
-R. of W.	399,906		
Special Cards			
- UK	198,464		
-Europe	201,897		
-U.S.A.	246,890		
-R. of W.	299,785		
Expenditure			
Printing			
- Material	74,789		
- Labour	61,890		
- Expenses	93,167		
Cutting			
- Material	71,789		
- Labour	58,625		
- Expenses	75,293		
Wrapping			
- Material	58,693		
- Labour	31,704		
- Expenses	34,471		
Packing			
- Material	38,568		
- Labour	36,906		
- Expenses	48,966		

Item 9 (for Task 5)

	PERFORMANCE REPORT PRODUCTION COST CENTRES TOTAL COSTS – AUGUST 20X3			
	\multicolumn{2}{c}{MONTH – AUG 20X3}	\multicolumn{2}{c}{YEAR TO DATE}	
	Actual £	Budget £	Actual £	Budget £
Material		108,500		341,700
Labour		32,250		198,500
Expenses		48,750		277,100

FTC FOULKS LYNCH

Item 10 (for Task 6)

COST / PERIOD	MONTH £	YEAR TO DATE £
Material		
Labour		
Expenses		

COMMENT

Item 11 (for Task 7)

SALES PERFORMANCE REPORT – AUGUST 20X3				
PROFIT CENTRE / PERIOD	MONTH ACTUAL	MONTH BUDGET	YEAR TO DATE ACTUAL	YEAR TO DATE BUDGET
	£	£	£	£
UNITED KINGDOM		98,000		785,000
EUROPE		109,000		832,500
U.S.A.		112,800		886,400
REST OF WORLD		142,100		1,164,600

Item 12 (for Task 7)

NOTEPAD

MOCK SIMULATIONS

Mock Simulation 1 – Questions

The situation

Your name is Melanie Rose and you work as an accounting technician for Blyth Chemical Ltd, an SME that supplies chemicals and cleaning materials to: farms, industrial units, public houses and shops together with a developing market in schools and colleges.

Your principal duties involve coding income and expenditure and preparing periodic performance reports on subjects as direct material, direct labour and overhead classifications. You are assisted in your work by a trainee, Mary Dunn, and you report to David Whitehead, the Management Accountant.

The time is late November – 20/11/X3 – and the firm has a year-end on 31 December. The activities take place between November 20th – 30th.

Blyth Chemical Ltd, has four main categories for its sales analysis:

- Farms
- Hotels, Public Houses, Shops
- Industrial Units
- Schools and colleges

Sales are analysed to the following responsibility centres i.e. sales areas:

- Scotland
- North of England
- Midlands
- South East
- South West

The cost centres include:

- Goods inward
- Storage area
- Goods outward
- Administration
- Sales
- Distribution activity
- Canteen
- Maintenance

UNIT 4 : SUPPLYING INFORMATION FOR MANAGEMENT CONTROL

The Coding System

The system is based on a three digit structure.

The first digit indicates the nature of the income or expenditure:

Cost centre expenditure

Responsibility centre income

Asset expenditure

Liabilities

Capital

Cost Centres

These are coded:

Goods inward

110	Storage area
120	Goods outward
130	Administration
140	Sales
150	Distribution activity
160	Canteen
170	Maintenance

The third digit denotes the type of expenditure:

001	Direct labour (sorting and packing)
002	Direct materials
003	Indirect labour
004	Indirect materials
005	Other overheads

Thus, some repair materials for the storage area would be coded 114

VAT is coded 180

       Input tax   01

       Output tax 02

Responsibility Centres

200	Scotland
210	North of England
220	Midlands

230   South East

240   South West

Categories of sale:

01   Farms

02   Public Houses/Shops

03   Industrial Units

04   Schools and colleges

Thus a sale to Newcastle College would be 214.

The company has a range of quality products:

Coded C1 to C10.

The contact details for Blyth Chemicals Ltd are:

Bawtry Road
Blyth
Nottinghamshire
S81 3KS
Tel. No: 01909 726132
Fax. No: 01909 726133
email: admin@blc.com
www.blychem.com

UNIT 4 : SUPPLYING INFORMATION FOR MANAGEMENT CONTROL

The tasks to be completed

Task 1 You receive the following memo (item 1) regarding the calculation of gross wages for the maintenance cost centre for week ended 30 November 20X3.

- Read the memo, calculate the wages and complete the coding, posting this to the coding extract (in item 6 of the answer booklet); and

- Prepare the analysis of maintenance hours spent per cost centre (using item 6 in the answer booklet).

Task 2 David asks you, once you have completed your labour analysis for the week, to prepare a report for management on the budget and actual labour cost per cost centre for the eleven months ended 30 November 20X3.

Use the report layout – item 7.

Task 3 Refer to the sales invoices on the following pages (item 2). Prepare the coding of these invoices and complete the coding extract (item 8a); and also the VAT coding (item 8b).

Task 4 David informs you that he is to be away at the month end and would like you to prepare the sales analysis report for the eleven months ended 30 November, for presentation at the monthly sales meeting to be held the first week in December.

Refer to the schedule (item 9) and your answer to Task 3 when compiling this report.

Task 5 David reviews your work from Task 4 and asks you to prepare brief notes on the performance of each sales area for the month of November (use the sheet in item 10 of the answer booklet).

Task 6 **Refer to the following purchase invoices (item 3) – they are all overheads chargeable to various cost centres.**

Code the invoices, post them to the extract shown (item 11); and complete the VAT coding in item 8b (partially complete in Task 3).

Task 7 Refer to the following petty cash vouchers.

You have decided to give the responsibility of coding petty cash vouchers to your assistant, Mary.

You are to code the six vouchers shown and explain in a few short notes to Mary, the reasons for the codes stated on these vouchers. Also complete the expenditure coding (item 12).

Task 8 David passes you an invoice coded earlier in the month (Item 5). He asks you to double check the extension and then write to the supplier for them to take the necessary action to correct this situation.

Item 1 Memo

To: Melanie Rose

From: David Whitehead

Date: 30 November 20X3

Re: Wages calculation of gross pay for the Maintenance Cost Centre

The gross pay calculations and cost centre coding for all cost centres are now complete, with the exception of the Maintenance Cost Centre.

The employees work a standard 38 hour week, any time over that is paid at time and a quarter.

You will find the details of hours worked, the nature of their work, the analysis of time spent and their rate of pay in item 6.

BLYTH CHEMICAL LTD   VAT No   279 98321
BAWTRY ROAD   Tel No   01909 726132
BLYTH, NOTTS   Fax No   01909 726133
S21 3KL   TAX POINT   30 November X3

SALES INVOICE

To: **No:** 1002
Stonehill Farms Ltd
Highland Drive
Huntley
Scotland H72 1JL   **Order No:** 8231

Details	Units	Price (£)	Total (£)
Agricultural chemicals Group C4 Size 4	5 packs	1,250.00 per pack	6,250.00
VAT			1,093.75
Total due			**7,343.75**

UNIT 4 : SUPPLYING INFORMATION FOR MANAGEMENT CONTROL

Item 2 Sales Invoices

BLYTH CHEMICAL LTD　　　　　VAT No　　　279 98321
BAWTRY ROAD　　　　　　　　Tel No　　　　01909 726132
BLYTH, NOTTS　　　　　　　　 Fax No　　　　01909 726133
S21 3KL　　　　　　　　　　　 TAX POINT　　31 November X3

SALES INVOICE

To:　　　　　　　　　　　　　　　**No:** 1003
Flyindales Farms Ltd
Bay Road
Flyindales
North Yorkshire YO21　　　　　**Order No:** 1276
3EJ

Details	Units	Price (£)	Total (£)
Agricultural chemicals Group C4 Size 8	10 packs	1,500.00 per pack	15,000.00
VAT			2,625.00
Total due			**17,625.00**

BLYTH CHEMICAL LTD　　　　　VAT No　　　279 98321
BAWTRY ROAD　　　　　　　　Tel No　　　　01909 726132
BLYTH, NOTTS　　　　　　　　 Fax No　　　　01909 726133
S21 3KL　　　　　　　　　　　 TAX POINT　　30 November X3

SALES INVOICE

To:　　　　　　　　　　　　　　　**No:** 1004
White Post Hotels
Highgate Road
London
W7 2PQ　　　　　　　　　　　 **Order No:** 1321

Details	Units	Price (£)	Total (£)
Cleaning materials Group C1 Size 10 (Group Hotel Purchase)	30 packs	1,200.00 per pack	36,000.00
VAT			6,300.00
Total due			**42,300.00**

MOCK SIMULATION 1: QUESTIONS

BLYTH CHEMICAL LTD 　　　VAT No　　　279 98321
BAWTRY ROAD　　　　　　　Tel No　　　01909 726132
BLYTH, NOTTS　　　　　　　Fax No　　　01909 726133
S21 3KL　　　　　　　　　　TAX POINT　30 November X3

SALES INVOICE

To:　　　　　　　　　　　　　　　**No:** 1005
South Down Inns Ltd,
North Bay
Taunton
Devon 　　　　　　　　　　　　　**Order No:** 1113

Details	Units	Price (£)	Total (£)
Cleaning materials Group C1 Size 5	4 packs	400.00 per pack	1,600.00
VAT			280.00
Total due			**1,880.00**

BLYTH CHEMICAL LTD 　　　VAT No　　　279 98321
BAWTRY ROAD　　　　　　　Tel No　　　01909 726132
BLYTH, NOTTS　　　　　　　Fax No　　　01909 726133
S21 3KL　　　　　　　　　　TAX POINT　30 November X3

SALES INVOICE

To:　　　　　　　　　　　　　　　**No:** 1006
Esk Valley Business
School
PO Box 62
Whitby
North Yorkshire　　　　　　　　　**Order No:** 722

Details	Units	Price (£)	Total (£)
Cleaning materials Group C5 Size 2	5 packs	30.00 per pack	150.00
VAT			26.25
Total due			**176.25**

FTC FOULKS LYNCH

BLYTH CHEMICAL LTD	VAT No	279 98321
BAWTRY ROAD	Tel No	01909 726132
BLYTH, NOTTS	Fax No	01909 726133
S21 3KL	TAX POINT	30 November X3

SALES INVOICE

To: **No:** 1007
Preston Engineering Ltd
Oldham Road
Preston
Lancashire M29 9QT   **Order No:** 997

Details	Units	Price (£)	Total (£)
Cleaning materials Group C9 Size 7	20 packs	40.00 per pack	800.00
VAT			140.00
Total due			**940.00**

MOCK SIMULATION 1: **QUESTIONS**

Item 3 Purchase Invoices

WHITBY TYRE COMPANY LTD SANDSEND LANE WHITBY YO21 3ZZ	VAT No Tel No Fax No TAX POINT	299 623171 01947 825430 01947 825431 30 November X3

PURCHASE INVOICE
No: 1731

To:
Blyth Chemical Ltd
Bawtry Road
Blyth
Nottinghamshire S81 3KL

Order No: 721

Details	Units	Price (£)	Total (£)
To Fitting 2 x 277 tyres to Delivery vehicle	2	141.00	282.00
VAT			49.35
Total due			**331.35**

B SMITH ELECTRICAL CARLTON ROAD WORKSOP NOTTINGHAMSHIRE S81 3EZ	VAT No Tel No Fax No TAX POINT	301 123727 01909 726431 01909 726432 30 November X3

PURCHASE INVOICE
No: 711

To:
Blyth Chemical Ltd
Bawtry Road
Blyth
Nottinghamshire S81 3KL

Order No: 727

Details	Units	Price (£)	Total (£)
Wiring materials (for repairs in good inwards bay)	1 pack	950.00	950.00
VAT			166.25
Total due			**1,116.25**

UNIT 4 : SUPPLYING INFORMATION FOR MANAGEMENT CONTROL

NOTTINGHAM OFFICE SUPPLIES LTD
MANSFIELD ROAD
NOTTINGHAM
NG21 3EZ

VAT No   921 673451
Tel No   0114 729677
Fax No   0114 729678
TAX POINT   30 November X3

PURCHASE INVOICE
No: 2001

To:
Blyth Chemical Ltd
Bawtry Road
Blyth
Nottinghamshire S81 3KL

Order No: 791

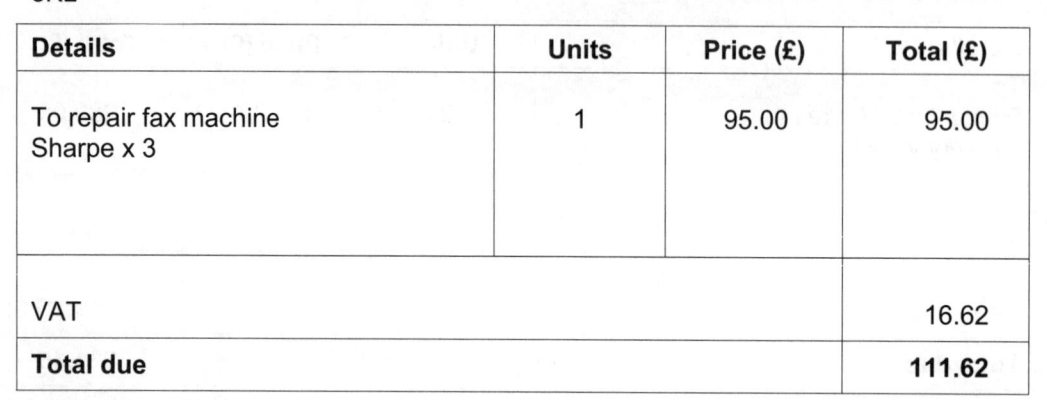

Details	Units	Price (£)	Total (£)
To repair fax machine Sharpe x 3	1	95.00	95.00
VAT			16.62
Total due			**111.62**

WELBECK FRUIT & VEG LTD
GATEFORD ROAD
WORKSOP
NOTTINGHAMSHIRE S81 7ZY

VAT No   976 273911
Tel No   01909 825111
Fax No   01909 825112
TAX POINT   30 November X3

PURCHASE INVOICE
No: 914

To:
Blyth Chemical Ltd
Bawtry Road
Blyth
Nottinghamshire S81 3KL

Order No: 798

Details	Units	Price (£)	Total (£)
To supply vegetables and Other items for w/e 30 Nov (Canteen)		92.50	92.50
VAT			
Total due			**92.50**

MOCK SIMULATION 1: QUESTIONS

NOTTINGHAM ELECTRICITY PLC
NEWARK ROAD
NOTTINGHAM

VAT No: 999 371721
Tel No: 0114 799399
Fax No: 0114 799300
TAX POINT: 30 November X3

PURCHASE INVOICE

To:
Blyth Chemical Ltd
Bawtry Road
Blyth
Nottinghamshire S81 3KL

No: 937

Order No: 811

Details	Units	Price (£)	Total (£)
To checking and verifying New electrical installation (Goods inward bay)		750.00	750.00
VAT			131.25
Total due			**881.25**

CLUMBER ESTATES LTD
CLUMBER HALL
WELBECK
NOTTINGHAMSHIRE S82 1LL

VAT No: 726 999721
Tel No: 01909 827211
Fax No: 01909 827222
TAX POINT: 30 November X3

PURCHASE INVOICE

To:
Blyth Chemical Ltd
Bawtry Road
Blyth
Nottinghamshire S81 3KL

No: 1174

Order No: 813

Details	Units	Price (£)	Total (£)
To rent of Administration offices Nov X1		350.00 per month	350.00
VAT			
Total due			**350.00**

BOB HEYES INSURANCE SERVICES	VAT No	996 991112
BAWTRY MARKET PLACE	Tel No	01302 551551
BAWTRY	Fax No	01302 550552
	TAX POINT	30 November X3

PURCHASE INVOICE

To: No: 1913
Blyth Chemical Ltd
Bawtry Road
Blyth
Nottinghamshire S81 3KL   **Order No:** 750

Details	Units	Price (£)	Total (£)
To insurance of office machinery Admin & Sales office (50:50) Per attached schedule	2	910.00	910.00
VAT			
Total due			**910.00**

TICKHILL MAINTENANCE SERVICES LTD	VAT No	299 623171
SUNDERLAND STREET	Tel No	01947 825430
TICKHILL	Fax No	01947 825431
DN1 93Y	TAX POINT	30 November X3

PURCHASE INVOICE

To: No: 3112
Blyth Chemical Ltd
Bawtry Road
Blyth
Nottinghamshire S81 3KL   **Order No:** 773

Details	Units	Price (£)	Total (£)
To supply maintenance Materials per attached schedule		590.00	590.00
VAT			103.25
Total due			**693.25**

Item 4 Petty Cash Vouchers

Petty Cash Voucher			
145		**No:** 111	
		Date: 22 Nov X3	
Details	**Unit**	**Price**	**Total**
Post Office Stamps Sales Office	100	27p	£27.00
Signature: M Dunn		Authorised by: M Rose	

Petty Cash Voucher			
135		**No:** 112	
		Date: 23 Nov X3	
Details	**Unit**	**Price**	**Total**
Newspapers & Journals Admin Reception area			£21.50
Signature: M Dunn		Authorised by: M Rose	

Petty Cash Voucher			
165		**No:** 113	
		Date: 25 Nov X3	
Details	**Unit**	**Price**	**Total**
Travelling expenses Interview for canteen personnel			£7.50
Signature: J Smith		Authorised by: M Rose	

UNIT 4 : SUPPLYING INFORMATION FOR MANAGEMENT CONTROL

145

Petty Cash Voucher			
		No:	114
		Date:	26 Nov X3
Details	**Unit**	**Price**	**Total**
Recorded delivery postal costs (sales office)			£14.50
Signature: *M Dunn*		Authorised by: *M Rose*	

135

Petty Cash Voucher			
		No:	115
		Date:	27 Nov X3
Details	**Unit**	**Price**	**Total**
Reimbursement of B&B overnight stay for D Whitehead Accountant	1	£44.65 *38-00*	£44.65 (incl VAT)
Signature: *M Dunn*		Authorised by: *M Rose*	

164

Petty Cash Voucher			
		No:	116
		Date:	30 Nov X3
Details	**Unit**	**Price**	**Total**
Various foodstuffs for canteen area	1	£48.00	£48.00
Signature: *P Drake*		Authorised by: *M Rose*	

Item 5 Purchase Invoice

WHITBY TYRE COMPANY LTD	VAT No	299 623171
SANDSEND LANE	Tel No	01947 825430
WHITBY	Fax No	01947 825431
YO21 3ZZ	TXT POINT	30 November X3

PURCHASE INVOICE

To: **No:** 1723
Blyth Chemical Ltd
Bawtry Road
Blyth
Nottinghamshire S81 3KL   **Order No:** 700

Details	Units	Price (£)	Total (£)
To Fitting 2 x 78 tyres to Vehicle M11 BLY	3	102.00	306.00
VAT			53.55
Total due			**359.55**

Mock Simulation 1 – Answer booklet

Item 6 (for Task 1)

Maintenance Cost Centre 170						
Employee	Rate of pay	Hours worked	Basic pay	Overtime	Gross pay
	£ - p	£ - p	£ - p	£ - p	
Brian Smith	8.50	44	323.00	63.75	386.75
Barry Curren	8.50	45	323.00	74.38	397.38
Jane Smith	7.50	43	285.00	46.88	331.88
Jack Jones	6.50	38	247.00	—	247.00
David Dunn (Supervisor)	9.50	38	361.00	—	361.00

An analysis of maintenance time spent per Cost Centre for the period was:

Employee	Hours worked	Cost Centre	
BJ	44	(100) 28 hrs (110) balance	16
BC	45	(150) 40 hrs (160) balance	5
JS	43	(120) 38 hrs (130) balance	5
JJ	38	(110) 2 hrs (150) balance	36
DD	38	overhead (170) 38 hrs	38

Cost Centre Coding   170

Gross pay
£
1724.01

£ - p

Total Basic Pay   1539.00
Total Overtime   £ 185.01

Cost Centre Analysis
Labour Cost Cumulative November 20X3 (nearest £)

Cost Centre	Cumulative Coding	w/e 30 Nov	To-date
	£	£	£
101	110,400	2,410	112,810
111	160,100	3,841	163,941
121	92,700	2,019	94,719
133	62,100	1,375	63,475
143	90,200	1,902	92,102
151	105,100	2,315	107,415
163	24,000	550	24,550
173	65,400	1724.01	67,124.01
	£710,000	16136.01	726,136.01

Analysis of maintenance hours per cost centre
w/e 30 November 20X3

Cost Centre	Maintenance hours Worked
100	28
110	18
120	38
130	5
140	0
150	76
160	5
170	38
	208 hrs

Item 7 (for Task 2)

Labour Cost – wages and salaries comparison budget to actual
for eleven months ended 30 November 20X3

Cost Centre Code	Budget	Actual	Variance F/(A)
	£	£	£
101	114,500	112,810	1690
111	161,000	163,941	(2941)
121	94,100	94,719	(619)
133	61,000	63,475	(2475)
143	89,850	92,102	(2252)
151	103,200	107,415	(4215)
163	24,100	24,550	(450)
173	65,200	67,124	(1924)
	£712,950	£726,136	£(13,186)

MOCK SIMULATION 1: **ANSWER BOOKLET**

Item 8a (for Task 3)

Sales responsibility centres Income Analysis November 20X3 (nearest £)

Code	Area	Cumulative to 23 Nov £	w/e 30 Nov £	Total to-date £
200	**Scotland:**			
201	Farms	124,500	6250	130750
202	Hotels/Public Houses/Shops	110,600	0	110600
203	Industrial Units	130,800	0	130800
204	Schools & Colleges	105,000	0	105000
210	**North of England**			
211	Farms	140,000	15000	155000
212	Hotels/Public Houses/Shops	125,600	0	125600
213	Industrial Units	131,100	800	131,900
214	Schools & Colleges	122,700	150	122850
220	**Midlands**			
221	Farms	99,500	0	99500
222	Hotels/Public Houses/Shops	121,300	0	121300
223	Industrial Units	141,700	0	141700
224	Schools & Colleges	137,200	0	137200
230	**South East**			
231	Farms	105,000	0	105000
232	Hotels/Public Houses/Shops	108,200	36000	144200
233	Industrial Units	117,600	0	117600
234	Schools & Colleges	121,750	0	121750
240	**South West**			
241	Farms	123,100	0	123100
242	Hotels/Public Houses/Shops	147,900	1600	149500
243	Industrial Units	131,250	0	131250
244	Schools & Colleges	127,650	0	127650
		£2,472,450	£59,800	£2,532,250

Item 8b (for Task 3)

VAT Analysis w/e 30 Nov

Code 180
 181 Input Tax   466.72
 182 Output Tax   10,465.00

FTC FOULKS LYNCH

UNIT 4 : SUPPLYING INFORMATION FOR MANAGEMENT CONTROL

Item 9 (for Task 4)

**Sales Analysis Report Comparative,
Budget – Actual eleven months ended 30 November X3**

Code	Responsibility Centre/ Area	Budget £	Actual £	Variance F/(A) £
200	Scotland	475,100	477,150	(2050)
210	North of England	525,000	535,350	(10350)
220	Midlands	510,000	499,700	10300
230	South East	451,100	488,550	(37450)
240	South West	535,000	531,500	3500
		£2,496,200	£2,532,250	(36050) £

Item 10 (for Task 5)

NOTEPAD

David

Please note the following comments on the performances as at 30 Nov X3

Scotland code 200, North of Eng 210 + S/E 230 all under performed

Midlands 220 + S/W 240 Both performed higher than budget

Regards Melanie

Item 11 (for Task 6)

Coding Sheet Purchase Invoices:

Supplier	Cost Expenditure Code	£
Whitby Tyre Company Ltd	155	282.00
B. Smith Electrical	174	950.00
Nottingham Office Supplies	135	95.00
Welbeck Fruit & Veg.	164	92.50
Nottingham Electricity PLC	175	750.00
Clumber Estates Ltd	135	350.00
Bob Heyes Insurance	135/145	910.00
Tickhill Maintenance Services	174	590.00
		4019.50

+ Sales Admin

MOCK SIMULATION 1: **ANSWER BOOKLET**

Item 12 (for Task 7)

**Petty Cash
Expenditure Code Analysis**

Voucher No.	Cost Code	Amount
111	145	27.00
112	135	21.50
113	165	7.50
114	145	14.50
115	135	38.00
116	164	48.00
VAT Input Tax	181	6.65
		£163.15
		163.15

R to K for notes to me?

Item 13 (for Task 8)

**Blyth Chemical Ltd
(suppliers of Agricultural and Cleaning Chemicals)**

Whitby Tyre Company Ltd
Sandsend Lane
Whitby
YO21 3ZZ

Bawtry Road
Blyth
Nottinghamshire
S81 3KS
Tel. No: 01909 726132
Fax. No: 01909 726133
email: admin@blc.com
www.blychem.com

Dear Sirs,

RE: INV No: 1723 ORDER No: 700

PLEASE COULD YOU SEND A CREDIT NOTE FOR £102.00 + VAT FOR OVERCHARGES ON THE ABOVE INVOICE (COPY ATTACHED)

Yours faithfully
Melanie Rose

FTC FOULKS LYNCH
159

Notes for Mary

Voucher 111 PO Stamps
              Sales Cost Ctr - 140
              Overheads   - 005
                           = 145

Voucher 112 - Admin Cost Ctr 130
              Overheads   - 005
                          = 135

Voucher 113 - Canteen Cost Ctr 160
              Overheads - 005
                        = 165

Voucher 114 - Sales Cost Ctr - 140
              Overheads   - 005
                           = 145

Voucher 115 Admin Cost Ctr - 130
             Overheads   - 005
                           = 135

Voucher 116 Canteen Cost Ctr - 160
             Indirect Labour = 004
                             = 164

Mock Simulation 2 – Questions

The situation

Your name is Andrew Fewster and you work as an Accounting Technician for Shireoaks Agricultural Engineering Ltd, a company specialising in fabrication, repair and maintenance work for the farming industry.

You report to the Management Accountant, Susan Woodhouse. Most of your work focuses on the monthly management accounting cycle. Your duties include coding income and expenditure for all source documents and preparing periodic performance reports. You are also assisted by a trainee Accounting Technician, John Brogan.

The company has four main sites which are classed as responsibility centres and include:

- Shireoaks, Nottinghamshire
- Epworth, Lincolnshire
- Carlisle, Cumbria
- Malton, North Yorkshire

The time is late January 20X3 and the company has a 31 December year-end. The company's finance function is centralised at Shireoaks.

The company has two main categories of business activity:

- fabrication
- repair and maintenance

Each site has productive Cost Centres; supported by a number of service Cost Centres; and include:

- machining
- fabrication
- repairs and maintenance
- administration (incl. Sales)
- stores
- maintenance (internal)
- canteen

The Coding System

The system is based on a six digit structure.

Sales income and expenditure is analysed by responsibility centre and type of business as follows; the first three digits indicate the responsibility centre.

Responsibility Centre

200	Shireoaks
210	Epworth
220	Carlisle
230	Malton

Type of business:

001	fabrication
002	repairs and maintenance

Thus a maintenance job in Carlisle would be coded as 220.002.

In the second group of three digits, the first digit indicates the nature of the income and expenditure:

1	Cost centre expenditure
2	Responsibility centre income
3	Asset expenditure
4	Liabilities
5	Capital

Cost Centres

These are coded as:

100	Machining
110	Fabrication
120	Repairs and maintenance
130	Administration (incl. Sales)
140	Stores
150	Maintenance (internal)
160	Canteen

The first and second digits denote the cost centre; and the third digit denotes the type of expenditure:

001	direct labour
002	direct materials
003	indirect labour
004	indirect materials (cost centres 100, 110 and 120 only)
005	other overheads.

Thus materials used on an order for some fabrication work at the Shireoaks unit, would be:

200.112

VAT is coded

170:   input tax 01

       output tax 02

The tasks to be completed

Task 1 Refer to the Sales and Purchase invoices following these tasks (item 1).

Prepare the coding of these invoices and complete the extract (item 4).

Task 2 Having coded the Sales invoices, you are required to complete the Sales Income Analysis for the period and then compare the budget with the actual showing the variances for each responsibility centre and in total.

Use item 5 for this.

Task 3 Having completed your sales analysis report – Budget to Actual for the period, you are required to calculate the percentage increase or decrease in sales compared to budget for each responsibility centre and in total; and summarise your results on the report (item 6).

Task 4 You receive the memo (item 2) regarding completing the salaries for the sales staff at each of the main sites.

Read the memo, determine the salaries, including the sales commission and complete the coding extract (item 7) together with a summary of gross pay.

Task 5 Following this assessment you will find the budgeted admin and sales department costs for the month of January together with the actual expenditure summary, with some entries posted (item 8).

Complete the report for the month.

Task 6 Having completed the analysis in Task 5, you are required to calculate the percentage increase or decrease in total admin/sales salaries for the month (item 9).

Task 7 Your company has a policy of maintaining a decentralised stores system with each centre being responsible for its own material issues.

Following this assessment you will find a series of material requisitions for w/e 31 January for the Malton site (item 3). Code these issues and complete the summary (item 10).

Task 8 You decide to pass the responsibility of coding petty cash expenditure vouchers to John Brogan. You are required to make a series of notes for John on the basis of the coding system and illustrate the application of the system to a petty cash expenditure voucher.

Item 1 Sales and Purchase Invoices

SHIREOAKS AGRICULTURAL ENGINEERING LTD THE ROW SHIREOAKS NOTTINGHAMSHIRE S81 8EZ	VAT No Tel No Fax No TAX POINT	278 42218 01909 812501 01909 812502 30 January X3

SALES INVOICE

To:
Collinson & Noble
Sandsend Farm
Whitby
North Yorkshire

No: 01/727

Order No: 713

Details	Units	Price (£)	Total (£)
To maintenance work Combine at Malton Shop per contract		1,650.00	1,650.00
VAT			288.75
Total due			**1,938.75**

SHIREOAKS AGRICULTURAL ENGINEERING LTD THE ROW SHIREOAKS NOTTINGHAMSHIRE S81 8EZ	VAT No Tel No Fax No TAX POINT	278 42218 01909 812501 01909 812502 30 January X3

SALES INVOICE

To:
Musgrave Farms
Harthill Lane
Kiveton Park
S89 3EP

No: 01/728

Order No: 127

Details	Units	Price (£)	Total (£)
To fabrication work on building at your property as agreed by Shireoaks Plant Staff		2,150.00	2,150.00
VAT			376.25
Total due			**2,526.25**

UNIT 4 : SUPPLYING INFORMATION FOR MANAGEMENT CONTROL

SHIREOAKS AGRICULTURAL ENGINEERING LTD
THE ROW
SHIREOAKS
NOTTINGHAMSHIRE S81 8EZ

VAT No: 278 42218
Tel No: 01909 812501
Fax No: 01909 812502
TAX POINT: 31 January X3

SALES INVOICE

To:
Dean & Smith Ltd
Cumbria Estates
Carlisle Lane Topp
P27 3EQ

No: 01/729

Order No: 621

Details	Units	Price (£)	Total (£)
To maintenance contract visit Corn drying equipment Carlisle Staff		950.00	950.00
VAT			166.25
Total due			**1,116.25**

SHIREOAKS AGRICULTURAL ENGINEERING LTD
THE ROW
SHIREOAKS
NOTTINGHAMSHIRE S81 8EZ

VAT No: 278 42218
Tel No: 01909 812501
Fax No: 01909 812502
TAX POINT: 31 January X3

SALES INVOICE

To:
Everatt Farms
Eastoft
Lincolnshire

No: 01/730

Order No: 1001

Details	Units	Price (£)	Total (£)
To fabrication work done to feed bins as agreed by Epworth Staff		1,150.00	1,150.00
VAT			201.25
Total due			**1,351.25**

MALTON OFFICE SUPPLIES　　　　VAT No　　　302 01721
PICKERING ROAD　　　　　　　　Tel No　　　01623 721962
MALTON　　　　　　　　　　　　Fax No　　　01623 721963
YO21 3EZ　　　　　　　　　　　TAX POINT　 30 January X3

PURCHASE INVOICE

To:　　　　　　　　　　　　　　　　　**No: 916**
Shireoaks Agricultural Engineering Ltd
The Row
Shireoaks
Nottinghamshire S81 8EQ　　　　　　**Order No: 224**

Details	Units	Price (£)	Total (£)
To repair photo-copier Malton office (sales office)		75.00	75.00
VAT			13.12
Total due			**88.12**

SCUNTHORPE OILS LTD　　　　　VAT No　　　317 826912
EPWORTH LANE　　　　　　　　Tel No　　　01732 459131
EPWORTH　　　　　　　　　　　Fax No　　　01732 459132
LINCOLNSHIRE LN1 3AB　　　　 TAX POINT　 31 January X3

PURCHASE INVOICE

To:　　　　　　　　　　　　　　　　　**No: 1521**
Shireoaks Agricultural Engineering Ltd
The Row
Shireoaks
Nottinghamshire S81 8EQ　　　　　　**Order No: 227**

Details	Units	Price (£)	Total (£)
To Three packs of Group 3 Cleaning Materials Size 7 for Canteen	3 packs	70.00 per pack	210.00
VAT			36.75
Total due			**246.75**

SHIREOAKS ROAD SERVICE STATION	VAT No	278 551127
SHIREOAKS	Tel No	01909 821201
NOTTINGHAMSHIRE	Fax No	01909 821202
S81 8EQ	TAX POINT	30 January X3

PURCHASE INVOICE

To:
Shireoaks Agricultural Engineering Ltd
The Row
Shireoaks
Nottinghamshire S81 8EQ

No: 01/9721

Order No: 221

Details	Units	Price (£)	Total (£)
To supply petrol for month Sales Staff cars Shireoaks main office	925 litres	0.70 per litre	647.50
VAT			113.31
Total due			**760.81**

CUMBRIA ESTATES	VAT No	307 26211
CARLISLE LANE TOPP	Tel No	01627 817211
CARLISLE P27 3EQ	Fax No	01627 817212
INVOICE:- 121	TAX POINT	30 January X3

PURCHASE INVOICE

To:
Shireoaks Agricultural Engineering Ltd
The Row
Shireoaks
Nottinghamshire S81 8EQ

No: 01/9721

Order No: 225

Details	Units	Price (£)	Total (£)
To rent of Carlisle Workshop 3 months ended 31 March X1	–	1,600.00 per litre	1,600.00
VAT			Zero rated
Repair & Maintenance shop			1,600.00
Total due			**1,600.00**

Item 2 Memo

To: Andrew Fewster, Accounting Technician

From: Susan Woodhouse, Management Accountant

Date: 31 January 20X3

Re: Salaries – Calculation of gross salaries for sales staff

I have prepared the salaries calculation for the salaried staff for January, other than those for the Sales staff.

The basic monthly salary for the sales personnel is as follows:

Brian Smith (Shireoaks Site)	£1,250
Richard Bows (Epworth Site)	£1,200
Malcolm Jessup (Carlisle Site)	£1,300
Steven Howe (Malton Site)	£1,200

In addition to the basic salary, each receives a sales commission of 3% of the monthly sales for their responsibility centre (to the nearest £).

Refer to your sales analysis for the period, calculate the commission and determine the gross salary for each salesman for the month.

Item 3 Materials Requisitions

MALTON SITE

Material Requisition			
Date: 22 January 20X3			No: 125
Details	Unit	Price (£)	£ - p
Galvanised hinges Size 1000	20	35.00 each	700.00
Signature: J Jones		Authorised by: B Barnes	
Fabrication Cost Centre		Job No 913	

Material Requisition			
Date: 25 January 20X3			No: 126
Details	Unit	Price (£)	£ - p
1 drum lubrication oil for machines	1	37.50	37.50
Signature: D Daws		Authorised by: B Barnes	
Machining Cost Centre		Job No 917	

Material Requisition			
Date: 27 January 20X3			No: 127
Details	Unit	Price (£)	£ - p
1 pack of cleaning materials	1	12.50	12.50
Signature: G Lloyd		Authorised by: B Barnes	
Canteen Cost Centre			

Material Requisition			
Date: 28 January 20X3		No:	128
Details	**Unit**	**Price (£)**	**£ - p**
5 metres of M.S. sheet size '003'	5 metres	70.00 per metre	350.00
Signature: *D Daws*		Authorised by: *B Barnes*	
Machining cost centre			

Material Requisition			
Date: 28 January 20X3		No:	129
Details	**Unit**	**Price (£)**	**£ - p**
1 starter motor 'XL 4' (repair to customer tractor)	1	165.00	165.00
Signature: *J Smithers*		Authorised by: *B Barnes*	
Repairs and maintenance cost centre		Job No 927	

Material Requisition			
Date: 30 January 20X3		No:	130
Details	**Unit**	**Price (£)**	**£ - p**
1 drum galvanised paint treatment (maintenance of customer premises)	1	85.00	85.00
Signature: *B Jones*		Authorised by: *B Barnes*	
Repairs and maintenance cost centre		Job No 928	

UNIT 4 : SUPPLYING INFORMATION FOR MANAGEMENT CONTROL

Mock Simulation 2 – Answer Booklet

Item 4 (for Task 1)

Coding Analysis Sheet
(Income rounded to nearest '£') for w/e 31 January 20X3

Code:	Value (£)
Income Analysis	
	£ _____
	_____
Expenditure Analysis	
	£ _____
	_____
VAT Output Tax	£ – p
171	_____
	_____
VAT Input Tax	£ – p
172	_____
	_____

Item 5 (for Task 2)

Sales Income Analysis for period ended 31 January 20X3 (to nearest '£')

Code	Actual to w/e 24 Jan	w/e 31 Jan	Total
	£	£	£
200.001	10,300		
200.002	17,250		
210.001	11,200		
210.002	12,100		
220.001	17,100		
220.002	15,250		
230.001	13,200		
230.002	14,950		
	£111,350		

Sales Income Analysis
Budget to Actual - Period ended 31 January 20X3

Code	Budget	Actual	Variance F/(A)
	£	£	£
200.001	10,500		
200.002	17,000		
210.001	11,000		
210.002	12,700		
220.001	17,500		
220.002	14,500		
230.001	13,150		
230.002	16,000		
	£112,350	£	£

Item 6 (for Task 3)

Percentage increase or (decrease) in sales over budget for period ended 31 January 20X3 (Calculate to 2 decimal places)

Code	% increase (decrease)
200.001	
200.002	
210.001	
210.002	
220.001	
220.002	
230.001	
230.002	
Net increase/(decrease)	_____ %

Item 7 (for Task 4)

Coding Analysis for Sales Salaries
January 20X3

Code	£
200.133	
210.133	
220.133	
230.133	
	£

Sales Salaries Summary
January 20X3

Responsibility Centre	Salesman	Basic Salary £	Sales Commission £	Total £
Shireoaks	B. Smith			
Epworth	R. Bows			
Carlisle	M. Jessup			
Malton	S. Howe			
		£	£	£

Item 8 (for Task 5)

Summary, budget and actual admin/sales expenses
January 20X3

Code		Budget £	Actual £	Variance F/(A)
200.133	(admin)	1,450	1,450	–
200.133	(sales)	2,050		
200.135		1,610	1,685	
210.133	(admin)	1,500	1,500	–
210.133	(sales)	2,000		
210.135		1,420	1,475	
220.133	(admin)	1,600	1,600	–
220.133	(sales)	2,100		
220.135		1,385	1,300	
230.133	(admin)	1,550	1,550	–
230.133	(sales)	2,000		
230.135		1,710	1,750	
		£	£	£

Item 9 (for Task 6)

	Budget	Actual	% increase (decrease)
Total admin/ sales salaries	£	£	£
	£	£	£

Item 10 (for Task 7)

Coding analysis, cost centre and cost code
Material requisitions - w/e 31 January 20X3

Code   £

Item 11 (for Task 8)

NOTEPAD

ANSWERS

Key Techniques – Answers

Chapter 1
Introduction to management information

Activity 1

The main purpose of financial accounting is to provide information on how the business has been run and how it has performed to parties external to the business. Financial statements, the balance sheet and profit and loss account, are prepared largely for the owners of a business, in a company this will be the shareholders, in order to show how the management have performed in the accounting period. The financial statements therefore show an historic picture of the business over the last financial year.

In contrast management accounting is designed to provide information for the managers of the business in order to help them to run the business more effectively. In order to be of use to management this information must be provided on a much more up to date basis than financial accounting statements. Typically management will require monthly, weekly and even daily information.

Financial accounting statements must be provided in a certain format laid out in the Companies Acts. However management accounting information can be provided in any format that is useful to management.

Management accounting information however must be much more detailed. Management will not only require information about total costs but also about individual costs for each product and the profit that each product is making. The financial accounting balance sheet shows a summary of the assets and liabilities of the business at the end of the accounting period. Management however will need constant information about assets such as stock levels. Financial accounting provides information about the business as a whole but management accounting information will need to be broken down into information about each cost centre or department of the business.

Activity 2

Decision-making

The management of a business will constantly be required to make decisions about the business. This may be day to day decisions such as how many production runs to make today or when to order more of a particular raw material. It will also include longer term decisions about how the business is to progress such as which products to continue and which to discontinue, whether or not to expand into a new factory, whether to invest in new machinery etc.

Planning

If a business is to be run successfully then there will be a great deal of detailed planning required. This will include long term planning such as when a new bank loan might be required and shorter term planning such as how many products to produce, what raw materials are required for this production and how many staff will be required in order to produce the items.

These plans, expressed both in physical and monetary terms, are known as budgets.

Control

Once budgets, or plans, have been determined then it is important that management can monitor how successful the business has been in sticking to these plans. Therefore actual results are compared to the budgets and any differences are investigated and changes made where necessary.

Activity 3

(a) The typical cost centres in a company which manufactures ready made meals might be:

- Preparation
- Packaging
- Distribution
- Stores
- Administration

(b) The typical cost centres in a hospital might be:

- Operating theatre
- X-ray department
- Ward 1, Ward 2 etc
- Accident and emergency
- Admissions
- Administration

Chapter 2
Coding of costs and income

Activity 4

Task 1

(a) 1120201

(b) 1224203

(c) 1821205

Task 2

A coding system has the following advantages:

(i) provides a quick means of referring to individual cost items;

(ii) reduces time involved in writing descriptions;

(iii) should avoid ambiguity;

(iv) should aid data processing, especially input of data.

Note: only two advantages were required by the activity.

Activity 5

Code 384 represents stationery used in the accounts department

Code 293 represents petrol used by the sales department

Code 172 represents packaging material used in the packaging department

Activity 6

Task 1

(a) (i) **Design principles**

(1) The system should be simple, logical and easily understood.

(2) It should be constructed to prevent duplication and to control the variety of stock items.

(3) The arrangement of code groups and sub-classifications should relate to the needs of the company.

(4) It should be flexible enough to incorporate changes in the pattern of materials stockholding without incurring a fundamental change in the coding system.

(ii) **Advantages**

(1) Each item of material is assigned a unique code, thereby reducing the risk of duplicating the orders for items with similar descriptions.

(2) Logical classification and coding assists the physical functions of storing and identifying materials.

(3) Grouping of related items and coding is inherent to computerisation of stock records and management reporting.

(4) Use of code, instead of a possible lengthy description, saves clerical work in preparing source documents and prevents ambiguity.

(b) It may be interpreted from the examples given that the materials coding structure represents

1st and 2nd digits	-	raw material, 01 aluminium to 04 stainless steel
3rd and 4th digits	-	length in 6" gradations
5th and 6th digits	-	thickness in $\frac{1}{16}$" gradations
7th and 8th digits	-	width in $\frac{1}{4}$" gradations

UNIT 4 : SUPPLYING INFORMATION FOR MANAGEMENT CONTROL

Task 2

Code number/fields

Material	Material code	Length (6")	Thickness ($\frac{1}{16}$")	Width ($\frac{1}{4}$")
Aluminium	01	13	04	14
Copper	03	02	06	13

Task 3

Code	Material	Length	Thickness	Width
01112903	Aluminium	5'6"	$1\frac{13}{16}$"	$\frac{3}{4}$"
03071721	Copper	3'6"	$1\frac{1}{16}$"	$5\frac{1}{4}$"

Activity 7

Task 1

(i) Boys shoes, brown leather uppers, rubber soles, size 4.

Code: 3 3 1 4 2 4 0

- Derived from second code illustrated in question
- Derived from first code illustrated in question
- As a half-size is shown in codes 1 and 2 in question 5, it is assumed 0 can represent whole sized

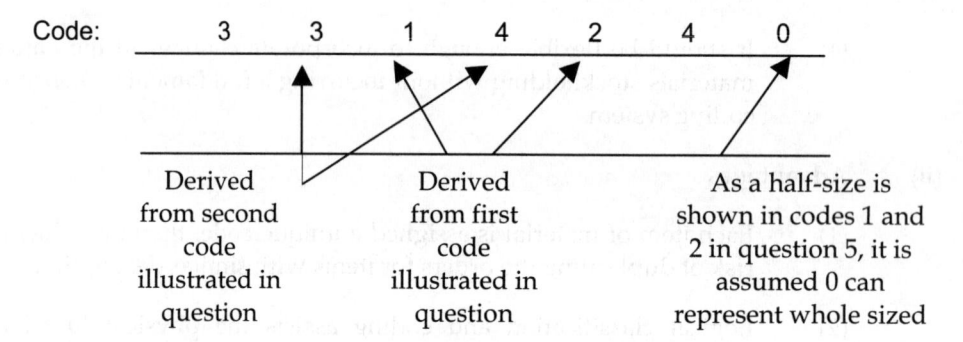

(ii) Ladies slippers, green felt uppers, rubber soles, size 4½.

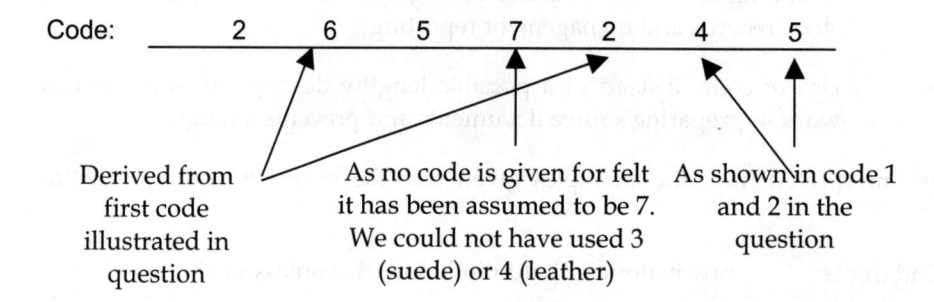

Code: 2 6 5 7 2 4 5

- Derived from first code illustrated in question
- As no code is given for felt it has been assumed to be 7. We could not have used 3 (suede) or 4 (leather)
- As shown in code 1 and 2 in the question

(iii) Girls shoes, burgundy leather uppers, leather soles, size 3½.

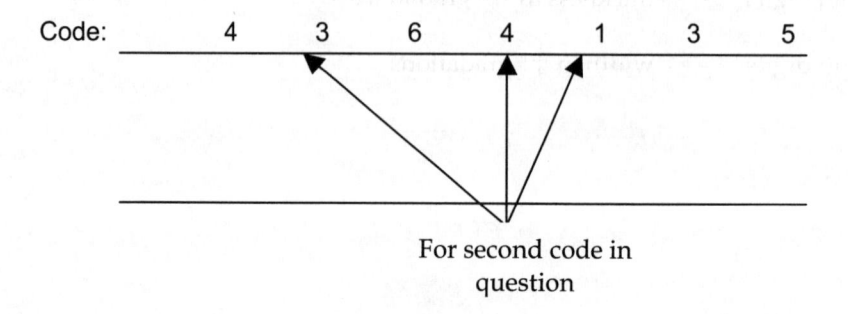

Code: 4 3 6 4 1 3 5

For second code in question

Task 2

A code is *a system of symbols designed to be applied to a classified set of items, to give a brief accurate reference, facilitating entry, collation and analysis.*

When designing a coding system the following principles should be borne in mind:

(1)   *Simplicity.* To ensure the code is easy to use - to minimise the likelihood of errors

(2)   *Unambiguity.* Each code should only refer to one item

(3)   *Flexibility.* It should be possible to add further categories

(4)   *Brevity.* Code should be kept short for ease of use and to reduce the chance of errors.

A coding system can have the following advantages:

(1)   It provides a quick, accurate way of identifying materials i.e. should avoid incorrect materials being issued to production or ordered from suppliers

(2)   It can provide a suitable basis for stores layout

(3)   It can reduce clerical effort by assisting in the sorting and preparation of reports for material control

(4)   It can assist in the computerisation of the materials control systems.

Chapter 3
Materials, labour and expenses

Activity 8

The documents used in the control and authorisation of materials purchasing procedures include the following:

(1)   Purchase requisition

(2)   Purchase order

(3)   Supplier delivery note

(4)   Goods received note

(5)   Purchase invoice.

Activity 9

£4.40 × 1.50 = £6.60

Activity 10

	£
Basic pay (47 hours × £4.26)	200.22
Overtime premium	
(9 hours × (£4.26 × 1))	38.34
	238.56

Activity 11

£10,000/15 = £666.67

Activity 12

Bonus (£22,000 × 0.02) = £440

Activity 13

Time based schemes, as the name suggests, involve the calculation of remuneration on the basis of time spent by employees and not linking that remuneration to productive work done or output produced. This will normally be at an agreed basic rate for a standard working week - in this case 40 hours. Hours in excess of this will then be paid as overtime at a higher rate. The existing scheme operated by A Ltd is an example - wages being paid at £4 per hour. It is also possible to incorporate premiums for shift working.

The advantages of time-based schemes are:

(a) they are appropriate for indirect workers;

(b) they should be used for direct operatives who cannot influence the rate of output - this is the case when workers are operating an automated or semi-automated production line or where team-working is necessary (an important feature of A Ltd is that the employees work independently which makes it feasible to introduce a performance-related scheme);

(c) they are most appropriate where quality of output is a key priority;

(d) the schemes are easier to understand and to administer.

Performance-based remuneration systems involve linking wages earned to the level of output produced. This may be done by basic pay being paid on a time basis and bonuses paid if output exceeds pre-determined targets. Alternatively a piece rate system can be used. In the case of A Ltd this is a differential piece rate system with a guaranteed minimum which is designed to protect employees' earnings from factors outside their control (e.g. stock-outs).

The main merits of performance-based systems are:

(a) less supervision should be necessary

(b) employees have an incentive to earn more in order to increase output: this increased output - assuming that it can be sold - will result in increased profit

(c) by spending less time per unit, savings should be achieved in other labour-related expenses.

A cost comparison can be made as follows:

Existing scheme

Output per employee	=	$\frac{6,000}{6}$
	=	1,000
Current basic wage per week	=	£4 × 40
	=	£160
∴ Average cost per unit	=	$\frac{£160}{1,000}$
	=	16 pence

Proposed scheme

Output per employee	=	$\dfrac{6{,}600}{6}$		
	=	1,100 units		
Expected wage per employee	=	800×0.16	=	128
	+	200×0.17	=	34
	+	100×0.18	=	18
				£180
Average cost per unit	=	$\dfrac{£180}{1{,}100}$		
	=	16.4 pence		

The proposed scheme offers employees the opportunity to earn at least the same amount per unit i.e. 16p but with potential to increase their weekly wage from £160 to £180. This assumes that the output level of 6,600 units is a reasonable estimate of what the employees can achieve. A potential problem with the scheme is that the guaranteed wage is effectively reduced from £160 to £140 which may not be acceptable.

Activity 14

Overhead:

Production	Selling	Admin	Financial
heat and light	telephone	rent	interest
power	postage	salaries	bad debts
supervision	sales commission	stationery	discounts allowed

Chapter 4
The selling function

Activity 15

In order for a department or part of a business to be treated as a profit centre it must have not only costs allocated to it, but also income.

The income of the sales department will be the net of VAT value of the sales that it makes. The department will also incur significant costs. These will in particular include the labour costs of the department. This will be the sales personnel's wages or salaries together with any commissions or bonuses that are payable. Other typical costs might be advertising costs and possibly packaging and distribution costs such as the costs of actually getting the products to the customer.

The sales department will also normally have allocated to it, its share of the joint expenses such as rent, rates, electricity etc.

However one of the main costs is likely to be the manufacturing cost of the goods actually being sold. If some figure for this cost was not included then the sales department would appear to be making huge profits therefore normally some figure for cost of sales is included.

UNIT 4 : SUPPLYING INFORMATION FOR MANAGEMENT CONTROL

This may be the cost accountant's figure for the manufacturing cost of the goods but it may also include a small profit element in some costing systems.

Activity 16

Sales coding listing

	To 23 June	Week commencing 25 June	Monthly total
	£	£	£
100400	9,320	3,644	12,964
100500	5,456	2,809	8,265
100600	10,429	3,259	13,688
200400	8,345	3,346	11,691
200500	3,104	1,188	4,292
200600	8,246	2,784	11,030
300400	7,245	2,745	9,990
300500	10,440	3,210	13,650
300600	7,324	2,513	9,837

Workings

Sales listings

Smarden outlet

	Mon	Tues	Wed	Thurs	Fri	Sat	Total	Code
	£	£	£	£	£	£	£	
Casual wear	340	558	610	442	513	883	3,346	200400
Business wear	120	140	155	254	189	330	1,188	200500
Sportswear	540	389	125	443	515	772	2,784	200600

Popham outlet

	Mon	Tues	Wed	Thurs	Fri	Sat	Total	Code
	£	£	£	£	£	£	£	
Casual wear	132	234	438	753	746	442	2,745	300400
Business wear	345	786	268	374	653	784	3,210	300500
Sportswear	218	765	498	431	276	325	2,513	300600

Yandle outlet

	Mon	Tues	Wed	Thurs	Fri	Sat	Total	Code
	£	£	£	£	£	£	£	
Casual wear	545	789	230	785	645	650	3,644	100400
Business wear	628	735	217	343	243	643	2,809	100500
Sportswear	507	836	367	431	653	465	3,259	100600

Chapter 5
Comparison of information

Activity 17

- A budget is a short-term manifestation of a longer-term plan.

- Variance:

The difference between the budget allowance for a level of activity and the actual cost incurred.

Activity 18
Hockeyskill Ltd

Sales report by region
Budget to actual for period ended 30 June

Region	Budget	Actual	Variance F/(A)
	£	£	£
Scotland & North	37,500	38,100	600F
Midlands	40,500	41,700	1,200F
South East	57,500	58,750	1,250F
South West	46,500	49,210	2,710F
	182,000	187,760	5,760

Activity 19
Northcliffe Feeds Ltd

Sales report by product
Budget to actual period ended 30 June 20X3

Production	Budget value	Actual value	Variance F/(A)
	£	£	£
A1 Plus	1,200,000	1,272,600	72,600F
B Plus	1,320,000	1,331,000	11,000F
Feed Plus	1,187,500	1,116,000	71,500A
	3,707,500	3,719,600	12,100F

Selling Price per tonne

	Budget	Actual	% increase (decrease)
		£ - p	£ - p
A1 Plus	100.00	101	1.00
B Plus	120.00	121	0.83
Feed Plus	125.00	124.00	(0.80)

Budget and actual production in tonnes for period ended 30 June 20X3

Product	Budget Tonnes	Actual Tonnes
A1 Plus	12,000	12,600
B Plus	11,000	11,000
Feed Plus	9,500	9,000
	-----	-----
	32,500	32,600
	-----	-----

Activity 20

	April 20X1 £	April 20X0 £	Difference £	Difference %
Materials	253,400	244,300	9,100	3.7
Labour	318,200	302,600	15,600	5.2
Expenses	68,700	72,400	(3,700)	(5.1)

Activity 21

	Budget £	Actual £	Variance £	Variance %
Cost centre 1				
Materials	48,700	46,230	2,470 fav	5.1
Labour	37,600	39,940	2,340 adv	(6.2)
Expenses	5,200	3,700	1,500 fav	28.8
Cost centre 2				
Materials	56,200	62,580	6,380 adv	(11.4)
Labour	22,500	20,400	2,100 fav	9.3
Expenses	4,800	5,600	800 adv	(16.7)

The two variances which are to be reported to management are the two expense variances.

Chapter 6
Reporting

Activity 22

(a) A report

(b) A note

(c) A memorandum

(d) A letter

(e) A memorandum

Chapter 7
Spreadsheets

Activity 23

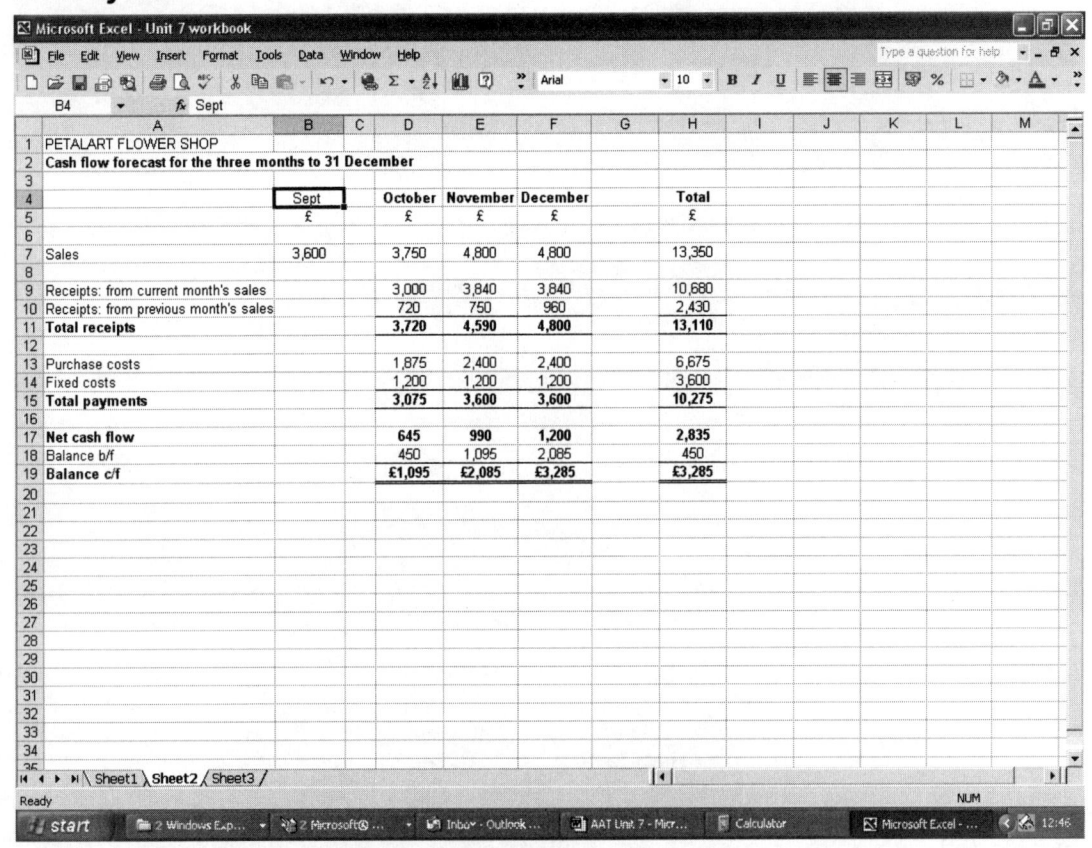

	A	B	C	D	E	F	G	H
1	PETALART FLOWER SHOP							
2	Cash flow forecast for the three months to 31 December							
3								
4		Sept		October	November	December		Total
5		£		£	£	£		£
6								
7	Sales	3,600		3,750	4,800	4,800		13,350
8								
9	Receipts: from current month's sales			3,000	3,840	3,840		10,680
10	Receipts: from previous month's sales			720	750	960		2,430
11	**Total receipts**			**3,720**	**4,590**	**4,800**		**13,110**
12								
13	Purchase costs			1,875	2,400	2,400		6,675
14	Fixed costs			1,200	1,200	1,200		3,600
15	**Total payments**			**3,075**	**3,600**	**3,600**		**10,275**
16								
17	**Net cash flow**			645	990	1,200		2,835
18	Balance b/f			450	1,095	2,085		450
19	Balance c/f			£1,095	£2,085	£3,285		£3,285

Note: formulae used (November column given as example)

E9:   = 0.8*E7

E10:   = 0.2*D7

E11:   = E9+E10

E13:   = 0.5*E7

E15:   = E13+E14

E17:   = E11-E15

E18:   = D19

E19:   = E17+E18

Practice Simulation 1 – Answers

Task 1

DATA INPUT SHEET
Sales invoices   Date: 9 June 20X3

			Coding	
Invoice number	Customer	Amount £	Revenue centre	Type of revenue
52711	Megabooks Limited	124.15	100	400
52712	Books Plus	103.80	100	500
52713	Empstone Books Ltd	145.80	100	400
52714	Win Hong Books	161.20	200	300
52715	Tradesales Limited	120.00	100	400
52716	Palmer and Company	299.52	100	400
52717	Business Books	148.40	100	500
52718	Megabooks Limited	228.80	100	400

Task 2

EMAIL

From: Parfraz Mehdi
To: Emily Padden
CC:
Subject: Checks on purchase invoices
Date: 9 June 20X3

Message

I have just checked a batch of purchase invoices. I have noticed the following discrepancies.

1. We have an invoice for £400 plus VAT from Editype Limited. I can find no purchase order corresponding to this. Please could you let me know if an order was raised.

2. We have an invoice from Litho Printing Ltd in respect of 5,000 copies of The Wars of the Roses. Only 500 copies appear to have been ordered (our order number 2271).

3. We have an invoice from Decofix Ltd for repainting the accounts office. This has been coded 660–710. I think it should be 660–720.

Task 3

DATA INPUT SHEET				
Payroll		Date:		9 June 20X3

		Coding	
Detail	Amount £	Cost centre	Type of expenditure
Gross pay	10,900.00	660	730
Employer NIC	967.95	660	730

Task 4

AVONTREE LIMITED PROFIT AND LOSS ACCOUNT

Date: 31 May 20X3

Account code	Account name	YTD This year	YTD Last year	Variance £	Variance %
100–300	UK sales: primary	75,600	74,100	+1,500	+2.0
100–400	UK sales: secondary	100,900	108,700	–7,800	–7.2
100–500	UK sales: higher	98,700	95,000	+3,700	+3.9
610–720	Typesetting: expenses	15,300	16,000	–700	–4.4
620–720	Editing: expenses	16,400	15,700	+700	+4.5
630–710	Printing & binding: materials	40,100	36,500	+3,600	+9.9
640–710	Distribution: materials	4,600	6,100	–1,500	–24.6
650–720	Marketing: expenses	16,400	15,900	+500	+3.1
660–720	Establishment: expenses	5,600	5,200	+400	+7.7
660–730	Establishment: salaries	34,200	33,000	+1,200	+3.6

Task 5

> **REPORT**
>
> **To:** Emily Padden
> **From:** Parfraz Mehdi
> **Subject: Variances YTD, May 20X3**
> **Date:** 9 June 2003
>
> ---
>
> I attach the schedule of variances, showing YTD figures to end of May for both this year and last.
>
> In the following cases the variances exceed 5% of last year's figures.
>
> - Account 100-400: down 7.2% on last year
> - Account 630–710: up 9.9% on last year
> - Account 640–710: down 24.6% on last year
> - Account 660–720: up 7.7% on last year.

Practice Simulation 2 – Answers

Tasks 1 and 2

**CODING EXTRACT – INCOME AND EXPENDITURE – AUGUST 20X3
(ROUNDED TO NEAREST £)**

Code	Balance (£)	Amendment (£)	Updated Balance(£)
111	38,916		
112	27,413		
113	33,476		
121	42,457		
122	29,376	1,700	31,076
123	24,294	3,800	28,094
131	38,461	1,600	40,061
132	34,761		
133	37,314	3,000	40,314
141	41,694		
142	52,316		
143	45,761		
211	47,412	750	48,162
212	11,467		
213	20,439		
221	43,764	890	44,654
222	11,461		
223	15,064		
231	8,216		
232	4,916		
233	9,074	1,500	10,574
241	3,642		
242	4,164	344	4,508
243	7,695	89	7,784
253	6,613		
263	7,008		
273	6,744		
283	4,539		

Task 2

PAYROLL CALCULATION AUGUST 20X3

NAME	John White
DEPARTMENT	Packing
BASIC RATE	£8.00 per hour
HOURS WORKED	43
HOURS FOR OVERTIME PREMIUM	8

	Calculation	Amount (£)	Code
BASIC PAY	43 × 8	344.00	242
OVERTIME PREMIUM	8 × 8 × 50%	32.00	243
EMPLOYERS PENSION CONT.	344 × 6%	20.64	243
EMPLOYERS N.I.C.	(376 – 84) × 12 ½%	36.50	243
TOTALS FOR POSTING	Code		Amount (£)
	242		344.00
	243		89.14

FTC FOULKS LYNCH

UNIT 4 : SUPPLYING INFORMATION FOR MANAGEMENT CONTROL

Task 3

MEMO
To: Liam Green   From: Candy Date   Date: 12 Sep 20X3   Subject: Invoice Coding
• I have received the invoices you passed to me for checking and wish to make the following observations.   • The invoice from Ince and Sons has been coded as s printing dept expense, however it was a charge for insurance for the factory as a whole. This needs to be apportioned to a range of departments and the basis for this can be discussed with Thelma, the management accountant.   • The invoice received from Aftercare Ltd was a invoice for a firm 'Cards Delight' in Portsmouth and not for our company. You need to draft a letter to them confirming the situation.   • The coding of the Cellplate Ltd invoice is correct, but there is an error on the invoice extension. Please check with the buying department, confirming the quantity ordered and the order price, before contacting Cellplate Ltd.

Task 4

INCOME AND EXPENDITURE BALANCES – Y/E 31/12/20X3

Ledger Account	Bal. At 31/7/20X3	Amt. Coded Aug 20X3	Bal. At 31/8/20X3
Sales	£	£	£
Birthday Cards			
- UK	245,365	38,916	284,281
-Europe	198,467	42,457	240,924
-U.S.A.	231,989	40,061	272,050
-R. of W.	297,946	41,694	339,640
Christmas Cards			
- UK	246,578	27,413	273,991
-Europe	316,578	31,076	347,554
-U.S.A.	297,697	34,761	332,458
-R. of W.	399,906	52,316	452,222
Special Cards			
- UK	198,464	33,476	231,940
-Europe	201,897	28,094	229,991
-U.S.A.	246,890	40,314	287,204
-R. of W.	299,785	45,761	345,546

Expenditure			
Printing			
- Material	74,789	48,162	122,951
- Labour	61,890	11,467	73,357
- Expenses	93,167	20,439	113,606
Cutting			
- Material	71,789	44,654	116,443
- Labour	58,625	11,461	70,086
- Expenses	75,293	15,064	90,357
Wrapping			
- Material	58,693	8,216	66,909
- Labour	31,704	4,916	36,620
- Expenses	34,471	10,574	45,045
Packing			
- Material	38,568	3,642	42,210
- Labour	36,906	4,508	41,414
- Expenses	48,966	7,784	56,750

Task 5

PERFORMANCE REPORT
PRODUCTION COST CENTRES TOTAL COSTS – AUGUST 20X3

	MONTH – AUG 2000		YEAR TO DATE	
	Actual £	**Budget £**	**Actual £**	**Budget £**
Material	104,674	108,500	348,513	341,700
Labour	32,352	32,250	221,477	198,500
Expenses	53,861	48,750	305,758	277,100

Task 6

DISCREPANCY (VARIANCE) REPORT
PRODUCTION COST CENTRES AUGUST 20X3

COST \ PERIOD	MONTH £	YEAR TO DATE £
Material	3,826 F	6,813 A
Labour	102 A	22,977 A
Expenses	5,111 A	28,658 A

UNIT 4 : SUPPLYING INFORMATION FOR MANAGEMENT CONTROL

COMMENT

The significant variances which are more than 10% from budget are:

Month variances:	Expenses	£5,111 A
Year to date variances:	Labour	£22,977 A
	Expenses	£10,002 A

Task 7

SALES PERFORMANCE REPORT – AUGUST 20X3

PERIOD / PROFIT CENTRE	MONTH ACTUAL £	MONTH BUDGET £	YEAR TO DATE ACTUAL £	YEAR TO DATE BUDGET £
UNITED KINGDOM	99,805	98,000	790,212	785,000
EUROPE	101,627	109,000	818,469	832,500
U.S.A.	115,136	112,800	891,712	886,400
REST OF WORLD	139,771	142,100	1,137,408	1,164,600

Task 8

NOTEPAD

Key points for telephone conversation with Sales Director:

- The report shows the performance relative to each profit centre
- It shows performance for current month and the year-to-date.
- Actual and Budgeted performance can be compared
- Variances are shown to indicate favourable and adverse positions
- Managers of the profit centres can be held accountable for the variances

Mock Simulation 1 – Answers

Task 1

Maintenance Cost Centre 170

Employee	Rate of pay	Hours worked	Basic pay	Overtime	Gross pay
	£ - p	£ - p	£ - p	£ - p	
Brian Smith	8.50	44	323.00	63.75	386.75
Barry Curren	8.50	45	323.00	74.38	397.38
Jane Smith	7.50	43	285.00	46.88	331.88
Jack Jones	6.50	38	247.00	–	247.00
David Dunn (Supervisor)	9.50	38	361.00	–	361.00
			£1,539.00	£185.01	£1,724.01

Cost Centre Coding	Gross pay
173	£1,724.01

	£ - p
Total Basic Pay	1,539.00
Total Overtime	185.01
	£1,724.01

Cost Centre Analysis
Labour Cost Cumulative November 20X3 (nearest £)

Cost Centre Coding	Cumulative	w/e 30 Nov	To-date
	£	£	£
101	110,400	2,410	112,810
111	160,100	3,841	163,941
121	92,700	2,019	94,719
133	62,100	1,375	63,475
143	90,200	1,902	92,102
151	105,100	2,315	107,415
163	24,000	550	24,550
173	65,400	1,724	67,124
	£710,000	£16,136	£726,136

FTC FOULKS LYNCH

UNIT 4 : SUPPLYING INFORMATION FOR MANAGEMENT CONTROL

Analysis of maintenance hours per cost centre
w/e 30 November 20X3

Cost Centre	Maintenance hours worked
100	28
110	18
120	38
130	5
140	-
150	76
160	5
170	38
	208 hours

Task 2

Labour Cost – wages and salaries comparison budget to actual
for eleven months ended 30 November 20X3

Cost Centre Code	Budget £	Actual £	Variance F/(A) £
101	114,500	112,810	1,690F
111	161,000	163,941	(2,941)
121	94,100	94,719	(619)
133	61,000	63,475	(2,475)
143	89,850	92,102	(2,252)
151	103,200	107,415	(4,215)
163	24,100	24,550	(450)
173	65,200	67,124	(1,924)
	£712,950	£726,136	£(13,186)

Task 3

Sales responsibility centres Income Analysis November 20X3 (nearest £)

Code	Area	Cumulative to 23 Nov £	w/e 30 Nov £	Total to-date £
200	**Scotland:**			
201	Farms	124,500	6,250	130,750
202	Hotels/Public Houses/Shops	110,600		110,600
203	Industrial Units	130,800		130,800
204	Schools & Colleges	105,000		105,000
210	**North of England**			
211	Farms	140,000	15,000	155,000
212	Hotels/Public Houses/Shops	125,600		125,600
213	Industrial Units	131,100	800	131,900
214	Schools & Colleges	122,700	150	122,850

220	**Midlands**			
221	Farms	99,500		99,500
222	Hotels/Public Houses/Shops	121,300		121,300
223	Industrial Units	141,700		141,700
224	Schools & Colleges	137,200		137,200
230	**South East**			
231	Farms	105,000		105,000
232	Hotels/Public Houses/Shops	108,200	36,000	144,200
233	Industrial Units	117,600		117,600
234	Schools & Colleges	121,750		121,750
240	**South West**			
241	Farms	123,100		123,100
242	Hotels/Public Houses/Shops	147,900	1,600	149,500
243	Industrial Units	131,250		131,250
244	Schools & Colleges	127,650		127,650
		2,472,450	59,800	2,532,250

VAT Analysis

Code 180 w/e 30 Nov
181 Input Tax £466.72
182 Output Tax £10,465.00

Task 4

Sales Analysis Report Comparative,
Budget – Actual eleven months ended 30 November X3

Code	Responsibility Centre/ Area	Budget £	Actual £	Variance F/(A) £
200	Scotland	475,100	477,150	2,050 F
210	North of England	525,000	535,350	10,350 F
220	Midlands	510,000	499,700	(10,300)
230	South East	451,100	488,550	37,450 F
240	South West	535,000	531,500	(3,500)
		£2,496,200	£2,532,250	£36,050 F

Task 5

Notes on Sales performance:

- The total sales for the period were 1.4% greater than budget.

- The North of England and South East sales were 2% and 8% greater than budget.

- The Midlands and South West's performances were adverse, being 2% and 0.7% less then the levels budgeted.

Task 6

Coding Sheet Purchase Invoices:

Supplier	Cost Expenditure Code	£
Whitby Tyre Company Ltd	155	282.00
B. Smith Electrical	104	950.00
Nottingham Office Supplies	135	95.00
Welbeck Fruit & Veg.	164	92.50
Nottingham Electricity PLC	105	750.00
Clumber Estates Ltd	135	350.00
Bob Heyes Insurance	135 ⎫	455.00
	145 ⎭	455.00
Tickhill Maintenance Services	174	590.00
		£4,019.50

Task 7

Petty Cash Expenditure Code Analysis

Voucher No.	Cost Code	Amount
111	145	27.00
112	135	21.50
113	165	7.50
114	145	14.50
115	135	38.00
116	164	48.00
VAT Input Tax: 181		6.65
		163.15

Notes for guidance for Mary:

- Voucher 111 post office stamps

    sales office cost centre 140

    overhead 005 - 145

- Voucher 112 admin cost centre 130

    overhead 005 – 135

- Voucher 113 canteen cost centre 160

    overhead 005 – 165

- Voucher 114 sales office cost centre 140

    overhead 005 – 145

- Voucher 115 admin cost centre 130

    overhead 005 – 135

- Voucher 116 canteen cost centre 160

    indirect material 004 - 164

Task 8

Letterhead:

Blyth Chemical Ltd
(suppliers of Agricultural and Cleaning Chemicals)

Whitby Tyre Company Ltd　　　　　　　　　　　　Bawtry Road
Sandsend Lane　　　　　　　　　　　　　　　　　　　　Blyth
Whitby　　　　　　　　　　　　　　　　　　　Nottinghamshire
YO21 3ZZ　　　　　　　　　　　　　　　　　　　　S81 3KS
　　　　　　　　　　　　　　　　　　　Tel. No: 01909 726132
　　　　　　　　　　　　　　　　　　　Fax. No: 01909 726133
　　　　　　　　　　　　　　　　　　　email: admin@blc.com
　　　　　　　　　　　　　　　　　　　　　www.blychem.com

Dear Sirs,　　　　　　　　　　　　　　　　　　30 November X3

Re: Your invoice 1723, our order 700

The above invoice received earlier this month for £359.55 was incorrectly extended. The order was for two Z8 tyres fitted to our vehicle M11 BLY, whereas the invoice showed a charge for three.

Could you please raise a credit note for £119.85 to correct this incorrect charge on the invoice.

We look forward to hearing from you shortly.

Yours faithfully,

Melanie Rose

MELANIE ROSE
Accounting Technician

UNIT 4 : SUPPLYING INFORMATION FOR MANAGEMENT CONTROL

Mock Simulation 2 – Answers

Task 1

**Coding Analysis Sheet (Income rounded to nearest '£')
for w/e 31 January 20X3**

Code:	Value
	£
Income Analysis	
200.001	2,150
210.001	1,150
220.002	950
230.002	1,650
	5,900
Expenditure Analysis	
200.135	648
210.135	210
220.135	1,600
230.135	75
	2,533
VAT Output Tax	£ – p
171	1,032.50
VAT Input Tax	£ – p
172	163.18

Task 2

**Sales Income Analysis for period ended 31 January 20X3
(to nearest '£')**

Code	Actual to w/e 24 Jan	w/e 31 Jan	Total
	£	£	£
200.001	10,300	2,150	12,450
200.002	17,250		17,250
210.001	11,200	1,150	12,350
210.002	12,100		12,100
220.001	17,100		17,100
220.002	15,250	950	16,200
230.001	13,200		13,200
230.002	14,950	1,650	16,600
	111,350	5,900	117,250

FTC FOULKS LYNCH

Sales Income Analysis Budget to Actual
Period ended 31 January 20X3

Code	Budget	Actual	Variance F/(A)
	£	£	£
200.001	10,500	12,450	1,950 F
200.002	17,000	17,250	250 F
210.001	11,000	12,350	1,350 F
210.002	12,700	12,100	(600)
220.001	17,500	17,100	(400)
220.002	14,500	16,200	1,700 F
230.001	13,150	13,200	50 F
230.002	16,000	16,600	600 F
	112,350	117,250	4,900 F

Task 3

Percentage increase or (decrease) in sales over budget
for period ended 31 January 20X3 (Calculate to 2 decimal places)

Code	% increase (decrease)
200.001	18.57
200.002	1.47
210.001	12.27
210.002	(4.72)
220.001	(2.29)
220.002	11.72
230.001	0.38
230.002	3.75
Net increase/(decrease)	4.36%

Task 4

Coding Analysis for gross Sales Salaries
January 20X3

Code	£
200.133	2,141
210.133	1,934
220.133	2,299
230.133	2,094
	8,468

Sales Salaries Summary
January 20X3

Responsibility Centre	Salesman	Basic Salary	Sales Commission	Total
		£	£	£
Shireoaks	B. Smith	1,250	891	2,141
Epworth	R. Bows	1,200	734	1,934
Carlisle	M. Jessup	1,300	999	2,299
Malton	S. Howe	1,200	894	2,094
		4,950	3,518	8,468

Task 5

Summary, budget and actual admin/sales expenses
January 20X3

Code		Budget £	Actual £	Variance F/(A)
200.133	(admin)	1,450	1,450	–
200.133	(sales)	2,050	2,141	(91)
200.135		1,610	1,685	(75)
210.133	(admin)	1,500	1,500	–
210.133	(sales)	2,000	1,934	66F
210.135		1,420	1,475	(55)
220.133	(admin)	1,600	1,600	–
220.133	(sales)	2,100	2,299	(199)
220.135		1,385	1,300	85F
230.133	(admin)	1,550	1,550	–
230.133	(sales)	2,000	2,094	(94)
230.135		1,710	1,750	(40)
		20,375	20,778	(403)

Task 6

	Budget £	Actual £	% increase (decrease)
Total admin/ sales salaries	14,250	14,568	2.23%

Task 7

Coding analysis, cost centre and cost code
Material requisitions w/e 31 January 20X3

Code:

230.104	37.50
230.112	700.00
230.102	350.00
230.122	250.00
230.165	12.50
	1,350.00

Task 8

Notes for John Brogan

John,

The following notes relate to the structure of the coding system and its application to coding petty cash expenditure, through analysing petty cash vouchers.

The coding structure is based on 6 digits.

- The company has four main sites: Shireoaks, Epworth, Malton and Carlisle.

The first three digits of the code relate to the location of the responsibility centre e.g.

Shireoaks	200
Epworth	210
Malton	220
Carlisle	230

The second group of three digits relates to the cost centre and the nature of the expenditure.

Each site has a series of cost centres, to which cost can be attributed:

- machining
- fabrication
- repairs and maintenance
- administration (incl. Sales)
- stores
- maintenance (internal)
- canteen

These are coded 100 through to 160 inclusive.

The classification of cost is listed below:

001	Direct Labour
002	Direct Materials
003	Indirect Labour
004	Indirect Materials
005	Other overheads

Thus, some materials used on contract for a customer at the Malton site, in the fabrication cost centre, would be:

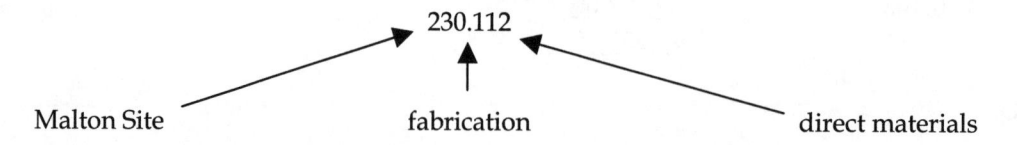

230.112

Malton Site → fabrication ← direct materials

Applying this to the analysis of a petty cash voucher we find:

Petty Cash Voucher

No: 711
Date: 27 Jan X3

Details	Unit	Price	Total
100 first class stamps for admin office Shireoaks site	100	0.27	£27.00

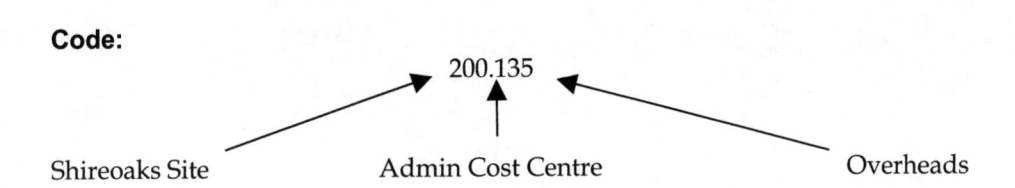

Signature: *J Brogan*   Authorised by: *S Woodhouse*

Code:

200.135

Shireoaks Site → (200) | Admin Cost Centre → (.1) | Overheads → (35)

- Shireoaks Site
- Admin Cost Centre
- Overheads

Index

Alignment 75
Automatic corrections 80

Bin cards 23
Bonus 31
Budgeted figures 52

Cell pointer 66
Clock cards 27
Coding of costs 13
Comparison of information 45
Confidentiality 54
Cost accounting 6, 7
Cost centres 8
Cost codes 13

Decision-making 4
Delivery note 22
Differential piece-work 30
Direct materials 26

Excel 63
Expenses 33

Financial accounting 5
Financial accounts 6
Format of a memo 57
Formula bar 64
Formulae 69

Goods received note 22
Goods requisition note 24
Goods returned note 24

Hourly rate employees 28

Indirect materials 26
Investment centres 9

Job sheets 27

Labour costs 26
Management accounting 6

Materials control cycle 20
Memoranda 57

National insurance contributions 31
Non-manufacturing organisations 32
Numbers 67

Output related pay 29
Overtime 28
Overtime premium 29

Pay of employees 28
Payment by results 29
Payroll 31
Piece rate with guarantee 30
Piecework 29
Planning 5
Point size 77
Profit centres 9
Purchase invoice 23
Purchase order 22
Purchase requisition 21

Reporting 56
Reports 58

Salaried employees 28
Scroll bar 64
Selling expenses 35
Service industries 32
Spreadsheet 62
Status bar 64
Stores ledger account 25

Time related pay 28
Time sheets 27
Toolbars 64
Typeface 77

Underlining 75

Word-processed documents 59, 77
Workbook 64

FTC FOULKS LYNCH

STUDY TEXT/WORKBOOK REVIEW FORM
AAT Unit 4

Thank you for choosing this FTC Foulks Lynch Study Text/Workbook for your AAT qualification. As we are constantly striving to improve our products, we would be grateful if you could provide us with feedback about how useful you found this publication.

Name: ....

Address: ....

....

Email: ....

Why did you decide to purchase this Study Text/Workbook?
Have used them in the past ☐
Recommended by lecturer ☐
Recommended by friend ☐
Saw advertising ☐
Other (please specify)................................

How do you study?
At a college ☐
On a Distance Learning Course ☐
Home study ☐
Other (please specify)................................

Within our AAT range we also offer Distance Learning Courses and Pocket Notes. Is there any other type of service/publication that you would like to see as part of the range?

CD Rom with additional questions and answers ☐
A booklet that would help you master exam skills and techniques ☐
Space on our website that would answer your technical questions and queries ☐
Other (please specify)..

During the past six month do you recall seeing/receiving any of the following?

Our advertisement in *Accounting Technician* magazine? ☐
Our leaflet/brochure or a letter through the post? ☐
Other (please specify)..

Overall opinion of this Study Text/Workbook

	Excellent	*Adequate*	*Poor*
Introductory pages	☐	☐	☐
Standards coverage	☐	☐	☐
Clarity of explanations	☐	☐	☐
Clarity of definitions and key terms	☐	☐	☐
Diagrams	☐	☐	☐
Activities	☐	☐	☐
Quick quiz questions	☐	☐	☐
Key technique questions	☐	☐	☐
Answers to key technique questions	☐	☐	☐
Mock exams/skills tests	☐	☐	☐
Layout	☐	☐	☐
Index	☐	☐	☐

If you have further comments/suggestions or have spotted any errors, please write them on the next page.

Please return this form to: Veronica Wastell, Publisher, FTC Foulks Lynch, FREEPOST NAT 17540, Wokingham RG40 1BR

Other comments/suggestions and errors

AAT Order Form

Swift House, Market Place, Wokingham, Berkshire RG40 1AP, UK.
Tel: +44 (0) 118 989 0629   Fax: +44 (0) 118 979 7455
Order online: www.financial-training.com
Email: publishing@financial-training.com

To order books, please indicate quantity required in the relevant box, calculate the amount(s) in the column provided, and add postage to determine the amount due. Please clearly fill in your details plus method of payment in the boxes provided and return your completed form with payment attached.

For assessments in 2005/06		Study Text		Workbook		Pocket Notes		Amount
FOUNDATION LEVEL								
Unit		Price £	Order	Price £	Order	Price £	Order	£
1, 2 & 3	Receipts, payments and an initial trial balance	20.00	☐	20.00	☐	6.00	☐	
		Study Text & Workbook						
Unit		Price £	Order					
4	Supplying information for management control	15.00	☐					
21, 22 & 23	Working with computers, personal effectiveness and health & safety	15.00	☐					
INTERMEDIATE LEVEL		**Study Text & Workbook**						
Unit		Price £	Order			Price £	Order	£
5	Maintaining financial records and preparing accounts	20.00	☐			6.00	☐	
6	Recording and evaluating costs and revenues	20.00	☐			6.00	☐	
7	Preparing reports and returns	20.00	☐			6.00	☐	
TECHNICIAN LEVEL		**Study Text & Workbook**						
Unit		Price £	Order			Price £	Order	£
8 & 9	Performance management, enhancement of value and planning & control of resources	20.00	☐			6.00	☐	
10	Managing systems and people in the accounting environment	15.00	☐					
11	Drafting financial statements (for December 2005 exam)	20.00	☐			6.00	☐	
11	Drafting financial statements (for June 2006 exam)	20.00	☐			6.00	☐	
15	Cash management and credit control	15.00	☐			6.00	☐	
17	Implementing auditing procedures (for December 2005 exam)	15.00	☐			6.00	☐	
17	Implementing auditing procedures (for June 2006 exam)	15.00	☐			6.00	☐	
18	Business taxation (FA04)	15.00	☐			6.00	☐	
18	Business taxation (FA05)	15.00	☐			6.00	☐	
19	Personal taxation (FA04)	15.00	☐			6.00	☐	
19	Personal taxation (FA05)	15.00	☐			6.00	☐	

* Pocket Notes for Units 1, 2, 3 & 4 are published in one book

TOTAL

Postage, Packaging and Delivery (per item):   Note: Maximum postage charged for UK orders is £15

Study Texts and Workbooks	First	Each Extra	Pocket Notes	First	Each Extra
UK	£5.00	£2.00	UK	£2.00	£1.00
Europe (incl Republic of Ireland and Channel Isles)	£7.00	£4.00	Europe (incl Republic of Ireland and Channel Isles)	£3.00	£2.00
Rest of World	£22.00	£8.00	Rest of World	£8.00	£5.00

Product Sub Total £...............   Postage & Packaging £...............   Order Total £...............   (Payments in UK £ Sterling)

Customer Details

☐ Mr   ☐ Mrs   ☐ Ms   ☐ Miss   Other ....
Initials:...............   Surname:...............
Address:...............
....
....
Postcode:...............

Delivery Address – if different from above
Address:...............
....
Postcode:...............
Telephone:...............
Email:...............
Fax:...............

Delivery please allow:–
United Kingdom – 5 working days
Europe – 8 working days
Rest of World – 10 working days

Payment

1 I enclose Cheque/Postal Order/Bankers Draft for £...............
   Please make cheques payable to '**The Financial Training Company Ltd**'.
2 Charge MasterCard/Visa/Switch/Delta no:

   ☐☐☐☐ ☐☐☐☐ ☐☐☐☐ ☐☐☐☐

   Valid from: ☐☐☐☐   Expiry date: ☐☐☐☐
   Issue no:
   (Switch only) ☐☐

   Signature:...............   Date:...............

Declaration

I agree to pay as indicated on this form and understand that The Financial Training Company's Terms and Conditions apply (available on request).

Signature:...............   Date:...............

Notes: All orders over 1kg will be fully tracked & insured. Signature required on receipt of order. Delivery times subject to stock availability. A telephone number or email address is required for orders that are to be delivered to a PO Box number.

Notes: Prices are correct at time of going to print but are subject to change